5/09

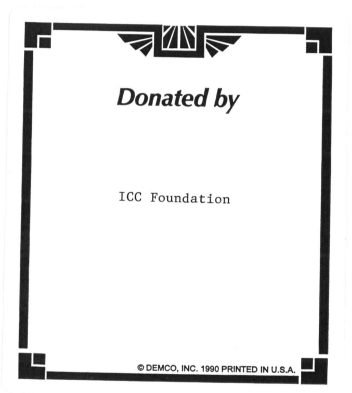

Donated by

ICC Foundation

Navigating the Financial Blogosphere

Navigating the Financial Blogosphere

HOW TO BENEFIT FROM FREE INFORMATION ON THE INTERNET

Russell Bailyn

John Wiley & Sons, Inc.

Copyright © 2007 by Russell Bailyn. All rights reserved.

Published by John Wiley & Sons, Inc., Hoboken, New Jersey.
Published simultaneously in Canada.

Wiley Bicentennial Logo: Richard J. Pacifico.

For general information on our other products and services or for technical support,
please contact our Customer Care Department within the United States at (800)
762-2974, outside the United States at (317) 572-3993 or fax (317) 572-4002.

Wiley also publishes its books in a variety of electronic formats. Some content that
appears in print may not be available in electronic formats. For more information
about Wiley products, visit our Web site at www.wiley.com.

Library of Congress Cataloging-in-Publication Data:

Bailyn, Russell, 1982–
  Navigating the financial blogosphere : how to benefit from free information on
the internet / Russell Bailyn.
       p.   cm.
  Includes index.
  ISBN 978-0-470-11810-8 (cloth)
  1. Finance, Personal—Blogs.   2. Investments—Blogs.   3. Retirement—
Planning—Blogs.   I. Title.   II. Title: Financial blogosphere.
  HG179.B2818 2007
  025.06'332—dc22

                                                                    2007011151

Printed in the United States of America.

10   9   8   7   6   5   4   3   2   1

To Evan and Bradley Bailyn,
the most talented entrepreneurs I know

Contents

Foreword

I

We're in the largest phase of technological growth the world has ever seen, and the tools we use to understand finance are new to many of us. The Internet is here. Information is disseminated quickly and conveniently, and educating oneself is easier than it has ever been before. However, with such a glut of information comes confusion. Even those who are on the cutting edge have difficulty in sorting through all of the masses of material published online every day.

For most, the best we can do is read the newspaper and skim through various web sites with the hope of grasping as much financial knowledge as possible. Those who are a bit more ambitious might go a step further and buy personal finance books such as this one. But how can we ever really feel satisfied that we've distilled all of this data into the strategies we need to be successful with money? Ultimately, the answer lies in filtering out superfluous information, and ferreting out as much meaningful knowledge as possible from the right sources.

Many of the changes that have taken place in the past 10 years could prove valuable from an investment standpoint—if you avoid the pitfalls. At a macro level, we've seen a move toward consolidation within the major stock exchanges. The conventional image of a loud, bustling trading floor is being replaced by the quiet whir of complex electronics that offer greater efficiency and pricing accuracy. And if you look carefully at the effects of fewer but larger stock exchanges, you can see a global marketplace on the horizon.

From a personal perspective, the choice of financial products just keeps on growing. An example of this could be the demand for exchange-traded funds (ETFs) that began earlier in this decade. ETF investing has garnered interest from both passive investors who enjoy low costs and transparency and more aggressive investors who haven't found success with active money management. The ETF is one of many financial products that provide investors with greater choices.

Further, one cannot help but notice the inclination toward debt that has grown in the past few years. Part of it is perhaps due to the low-interest-rate environment that began after the millennium in 2001 to quell the jitters created by the bursting tech bubble and the attacks of 9/11. Investors seem as willing as ever to take risks. However, risk is not so easily quantified. For instance, the housing market, which has traditionally been a safe place to park money and invest, has become (whether or not it should be) a complicated financial instrument. This became evident at the start of 2007 with a series of concerns about subprime lending and related risks. This sort of speculation presents real dangers, often to people who don't have a proper understanding of their own mortgages.

Many of these recent changes create incredible financial opportunities for the small subset of individuals who take the time to learn how to capitalize on them. Unfortunately, not everyone has the same motivation and passion for finance that I do. The majority of people remain uninformed regarding personal finance and investing. Even those who have done well for themselves remain in the dark about modern financial basics.

II

As this book describes, improved communication can ultimately lead investors to greater success with their money. We should embrace the transfer of information and try to identify that which is of value to us. This book will help you do that, and simultaneously introduce you to the "blog." If you take the time to visit the various web references mentioned herein, you will no doubt increase your financial savvy and feel more confident in your money-related decisions.

I've known Russell for several years now, mostly through his dedicated involvement with Jewish Heritage Programs. He has a real aptitude for transferring his own understandings clearly and intelligently. His success as a financial planner is reassurance that one should feel safe with him as a guide to the investing blogosphere. After reading this book, you will be able to make better sense of the wealth of financial knowledge available on the Internet—and, one hopes, make practical use of it.

MICHAEL STEINHARDT

Michael Steinhardt is a legendary investor. He retired from active money management in 1995 and has since devoted himself to philanthropy. His autobiography, *No Bull: My Life In and Out of Markets*, was published by John Wiley & Sons in 2001.

Preface

I made an observation earlier this year that the vast majority of personal finance books that cross my desk fall into the same few categories. Some offer the so-called solution to becoming rich, generally through a specific formula of investments that supposedly can't be beat. I've read a bunch of these, some of which have really influenced my thoughts, but the majority of which continue to dress up my bookshelf.

Other books talk about low-cost methods of investing, and why many investors who ultimately find success are passive rather than active with their financial decisions. These books are often characterized by broker bashing, a practice that stems from the belief that many stockbrokers and financial advisers not only lack value, but can ultimately be detrimental to one's financial health.

If the book doesn't fit into one of these two categories, it's probably exposing a concept that could be summed up in a few paragraphs but instead is stretched out over 200 pages. If you're listening now, it's probably because you recognize what I'm saying as true.

The defining traits of my book are not how it can make you a quick fortune or enable you to instantly become a self-sufficient investor. I don't believe either of those goals is realistic. My book is about communication, and the lack thereof that creates difficulty for the millions of people trying to find adequate and unbiased financial information. I start at the beginning of a typical personal finance journey by answering basic questions such as how to choose a bank and how to read a credit score. I then venture on to the saving and investment questions that most people field in their working years. We finish with a discussion of longer-term financial issues, such as retirement and Social Security, which many of us will grapple with.

The chapter topics were selected from a pool of questions I actually received from readers of my blog (www.russellbailyn.com/weblog). By organizing the book this way, I'm trying to respond to the needs of a very broad range of people. Some of these people already have knowledge about personal finance, while others are beginners. I think organizing the book this way is an improvement upon the more traditional format of having an expert determine what you should know and then write about it. This concept of bottom-up information is embedded in the culture of blogging. We'll talk more about this in the Introduction.

Most of the chapters are designed as a series of questions, with subheadings to address the specific issues within each topic. I wrote the chapters in short, digestible segments so that the content remains fresh and the concepts actually stick. This way, you can apply the knowledge to your everyday financial life. I like to chop up personal finance into the smallest possible pieces as a response to the multitude of financial literature I've read that is quite the opposite: long and full of confusing terminology. Authors who write like this do themselves a huge disservice. While the content is often unique and valuable, readers become alienated by the financial jargon and often never even finish reading. I didn't want this to happen with my book. The way I see it, the faster you finish reading, the sooner you can move on to the more important goal: feeling comfortable about your personal financial life.

Russell Bailyn

New York, New York
August 2007

Acknowledgments

Writing a book is a bittersweet experience. When it's finished and available for purchase, the focus has already shifted from writing the book to selling it. However, to truly understand the combination of efforts that go into producing a book, it would be more appropriate if it were sold as hundreds of sheets of paper scattered in piles with paper clips, highlighting, and various markings. In the past few months, I've seen my desk crowded to the point that I'd place a client on hold for several minutes before being able to locate a file or particular document.

Needless to say, there were several people without whom this book project might never have come to fruition.

The editing and production teams at John Wiley & Sons, Inc., were incredible. Infinite thanks to Bill Falloon, Laura Walsh, and Emilie Herman for their support. In terms of providing wisdom and advice for each chapter, a debt of gratitude goes out to the team I work with at Premier Financial Advisors—I couldn't have asked for more knowledgeable and talented colleagues. I'd like to give special thanks to John Diaz, the founder and CEO of our firm. He has been my trusted mentor for years, and I owe much of my success to his unrelenting support of my endeavors. I'd also like to thank Fred Swain, Rachel Segall, Brad Carey, and Stacey Du. Each of these people offers knowledge and support to me on a daily basis. Next, what would I do without the bloggers? To every person out there who stays up late sharing insight and research with the rest of us in the blogosphere, I appreciate your contributions. You have been my inspiration for this unique project.

At a more personal level, it would have been considerably more difficult to finish this project without the encouragement and insight of my closest friends, particularly Theodore Phillips, Natalie Rubinstein, Nora Sverdlov, Ben Margolis, and Eitan Bouskila. A special thanks to Stephanie Langsner for sharing this important phase of life with me. She now has a deeper knowledge of financial planning than she ever bargained for. Her patience and tolerance have been remarkable.

In terms of emotional support, which becomes extremely important during long days and nights of writing, I can't thank my family enough. I also appreciate their good humor in letting me use them as examples in the book. Thanks, guys.

R.B.

About the Author

Russell Bailyn is a wealth manager with Premier Financial Advisors, an independent financial planning and investment advisory firm located in New York City. He is also a registered representative with First Allied Securities, Inc., a NASD/SIPC member broker/dealer firm.

Russell is also an active member of the Financial Planning Association, an organization dedicated to professional development and career management, and a contributing member of the Seeking Alpha network, a blog aggregator service.

Russell's positioning as a blogger with a fresh perspective on financial planning has landed him features in *Wealth Manager* magazine and *Financial Advisor* magazine. He has also been publicized online, including mentions on About.com, TheStreet.com, and Advisor.ca.

Russell received a bachelor of science degree from New York University in communication studies in May 2004. He is currently enrolled in the Certified Financial Planner (CFP) certificate program, also at New York University.

Introduction: Why Navigate the Blogosphere?

Bloggers strive to connect people with the best information possible. One way to accomplish such a task is by forming a community in which to share thoughts and opinions. This collective wisdom should make arriving at decisions considerably easier. You may even find that reading blogs provides you with a fresh perspective that improves upon more traditional media outlets such as television.

At this point you may be thinking, "Blogging? What does this have to do with finance and investing?" Many people still think of blogs strictly in terms of reading about politics. Granted, politics was among the early topics to be found in the blogosphere and continues to dominate. However, as the blog medium continues to gain recognition, many other topics are entering the scene as well.

I've found that reading blogs can be particularly beneficial to people seeking financial advice. All too often we trust the insight of so-called experts when it comes to managing our money and helping us make financial decisions. The problem is that many of these experts are driven by a profit motive, which leads to distorted information. Other experts have become too comfortable with the idea of giving the same advice to different groups of people. This is ironic in that finance is a very subjective topic. Many financial issues boil down to a few simple rules coupled with a solid understanding of one's own personal preferences.

My own experience with blogging dates back to the 2004 presidential elections. It was unconfirmed who would get the electoral votes for Ohio, and I thought involving myself in the action would be more exciting than going to sleep. Because of the scramble for constantly updated information, all eyes were on the blogosphere. In my experience, this was the first time the Internet had become a competing outlet for information over television. I remember viewing that night as a sign of the times. I started to read a handful of blogs each day in addition to my existing routine of the *Wall Street Journal* and Yahoo! Finance.

Shortly after that election, I was chatting with my brother Brad about marketing tools we use to attract clients. Brad pointed out that high placement on search engines seemed to bring in steady business for his new ghostwriting service. I thought this was particularly interesting, given that the Internet was perhaps the last place I would have thought of to market financial planning services. Brad suggested that I start by creating an identity for myself online. We decided a blog would be a better choice than a traditional web site because it allows for users to leave feedback. This way, we thought, visitors who enjoyed the content would leave comments, come back to visit, and participate in discussions. This was my experience with other blogs, so I would try to do the same thing.

Needless to say, by the end of 2005 I had become a blogger. My friends laughed at first, as did I sometimes. Fewer people are laughing now, as the blog (www.russellbailyn.com/weblog) has been a boon to both my financial planning practice and (believe it or not) my social life. In fact, I've convinced many people, including those with very little inclination toward technology, to start their own blogs.

What Exactly *Is* a Blog?

A blog (short for web log) is a collection of entries that is published online to reflect the attitudes and thoughts of the author. You may notice that many blogs have a catchy title and/or subtitle. I will point out the names of many blogs referenced in the following chapters in addition to providing you with the web address. I'm actually an exception to this rule in that my title is a straightforward description of my blog (Russell Bailyn's Financial Planning Blog). This serves two purposes in my case: It brands my name—one of the original goals when I started the blog—and it optimizes my site for keywords such as *financial, planning,* and *blog,* all terms that enable people to find me and my services when using search engines.

Blog content is usually organized by date, with the most recent entry at the top. Links, comments, images, and advertisements are often built into and around the discussions. The goal of including these features is to create a community-like atmosphere in which users can become interested and participate in the various discussions that intrigue them. They can leave comments or questions on the site and often e-mail the blogger directly as well. Some blogs are text-based, focusing on specific topics such as financial planning or foreign policy. Others are primarily collections of links, pictures, or thoughts, all of which usually revolve around a theme.

My own blog takes on a rather simple format. I use Moveable Type, which is a personal publishing platform designed to conveniently organize and access information. Besides the user-friendly format, I also chose this blogging platform because, once the software is installed, all the user needs to do is write their thoughts and click Publish. Since most of us aren't overly savvy when it comes to technology, the blogging format should prove to be a comfortable and convenient environment for even the internet-phobic.

You'll notice references to various blogs found at the end of each chapter. I selected these bloggers based on their commitment to the characteristics that make for a good blog. This includes unique content, frequent updates (at least once per week if not every day), and active interaction with readers. I tried to vary the blogging personalities I chose to keep your visits as interesting as possible. My hope is that you'll find the time to turn on your computer and navigate the blogosphere on your own.

Why Are Blogs Becoming So Popular?

Blogging integrates communication and information in a very real way. It has often been compared to innovations such as instant messaging and e-mailing in the ways it affects people. Among the various explanations for why blogging is quickly becoming a preferred source for information is that bloggers cut and paste information from various sources and link to it on their sites. This, as opposed to receiving all of one's information from a single source, allows for you to compare, contrast, and ponder various bits of information.

Meanwhile, the exact opposite has happened in more traditional media outlets. Objectivity and accuracy have taken a backseat to (what else?) money. So many choices have become available in the world of television that a network must home in on a specific market to keep its identity and strengthen its fan base. The downside to such competition is that a struggle emerges to air something different from the next network's programming to keep information new and interesting. The result is often sensationalist programming and news that is driven by anything but objectivity.

Whereas many of the early blogs originated in the political arena, we're seeing blogs covering a wide variety of topics on the Internet today. I find personal finance and investing to be great opportunities for bloggers since many financial concepts seem to be widely misunderstood and in need of more attention. Furthermore, I've found that information and advice offered by nonprofessionals is often just as valuable as what the experts have to say. I don't believe in one specific methodology that everyone can follow to get ahead financially. Reading blogs has improved the advice I give to my clients and introduced me to countless other resources for information. I hope it can do the same for you.

A Brief Disclaimer

I'm hoping you won't encounter many inactive links or missing web pages, or much inaccurate content, when you visit the various blog and Internet references. I contacted most of the included bloggers sometime during late 2006 and early 2007 to confirm that they would still be actively blogging in the foreseeable future. While nearly all said yes and were excited about inclusion in the book, life can throw us curveballs. Sometimes a blogger will shut down a site, merge it with another, sell it, or encounter some other situation that is hard to anticipate a year in advance. It should go without saying that I can't ensure the accuracy of the content posted on each and every site. I tried to choose people who, based on my experience, are knowledgeable and post accurate information. However, one should always try to confer with a professional when making financial decisions. If you stop by my blog from time to time, I will post updates on any changes regarding information provided in the book. I'd also love to chat with readers who offer comments or questions about any of the topics found within.

In the interest of full disclosure, I'd also like to touch briefly on my day job. I work for Premier Financial Advisors, an independent financial planning and investment advisory firm located in New York City. As I am also a licensed advisor with First Allied Securities, Inc. (Series 7, 63, and 65), it must be clear that this book was written as an informational resource and not as an endorsement of any particular product or strategy. With that said, enjoy the book!

PART

I

FIRST PERSPECTIVES ON MONEY

CHAPTER 1

How Do I Choose a Bank?
Does It Really Matter?

Just like you or I have a home, so does our money. It's known as a bank, and is among the fundamental institutions of modern society. Our money waits there, ready to be spent, and often builds up interest in the meanwhile. Checking account funds can be accessed in a variety of convenient ways, including automatic debits and check writing. You can also use your automated teller machine (ATM) card to make a purchase or to withdraw cash from a machine. Being inside a bank is also a sensory experience. There are bundles of money all over the place, safe-deposit boxes where valuables can be stored, and convenient coin-counting machines. Many banks also have associates standing by to assist you in borrowing money on short notice to purchase a home, a car, an education, or another item that you either can't afford to pay for up front or don't desire to for some reason.

These are some of the qualities I think of when picturing a bank. However, not all banks are the same. Whereas most generate revenue through variations of the same few processes, each bank generally has its own culture that can differ quite widely from the next. Understanding some of these similarities and differences can teach you what to look for when doing your own banking and make you a wiser consumer overall. We'll discuss some of these issues.

What Makes a Bank *Good*?

People generally look for banks that are close to their homes or offices. You probably wouldn't want to keep your money somewhere that it became difficult to access. Hours of operation may be important to you as well. If you do business with one of those banks that close at 2:00 P.M. on weekdays and that don't open at all on the weekends, banking becomes extremely inconvenient. That's certainly not necessary anymore. Competition has improved these kinds of problems, and now many banks are open until 7:00 P.M. on weekdays, most banks have Saturday hours, and some are open on Sundays as well.

You may notice that most banks are open, airy, and luxurious. Due to the sensitivity people feel about their money, it's crucial that banks carefully consider the message given by their atmosphere. A bank that is cluttered, dark, and disorganized probably wouldn't appeal to a very desirable clientele. I find this analogous to my own firm's office in New York City. Because we handle personal finances, our offices must exude prosperity. Our location is quite expensive, conveniently located in the heart of Fifth Avenue shopping and a short skip from Central Park. Could we practice financial planning from elsewhere? Sure, but image is important, especially in finance and banking.

A bank can achieve a competitive edge by offering exceptional features to its customers. For example, some banks offer free checking without any minimum-balance requirements if you establish direct deposit. Direct deposit, for those who aren't familiar with it, refers to some form of payment that gets automatically deposited into your bank account, usually once or twice a month. Banks like direct deposit because it provides stability of cash flow, which can be used to improve record keeping and ultimately make the lending process more reliable.

Online banking has become the bank feature of choice in the twenty-first century. Why leave your home or office if you don't have to? You can monitor transactions online, view monthly statements, transfer money from savings to checking, pay bills using various payment links, or even stop a check. The only thing you can't do is request a bundle of cash to eject itself from your screen. Often visiting a bank's web site will fill you in about online capabilities.

Some banks offer insurance and investment products in addition to their other accounts and services. Unless you're dealing specifically with an arm of the bank that offers comprehensive financial planning services, the bank will not be your best bet for these products. Most banks work strictly on commission, which can lead to recommendations that aren't always in the best interests of the client.

Banks earn money from fees they charge for personal banking. If you're a very attentive consumer, you will ask for a copy of your bank's fee schedule either when you first open your account or soon afterward. This way you can see how your bank's fees stack up against others' fees. You can probably even find these fee schedules on the bank's web site. The most common fees I've found are for wire transfers, stop payments, insufficient funds, and official checks. Banks sometimes have service charges as well, which are different from fees. An example is a monthly maintenance expense, which covers operational costs such as printing and sending monthly statements.

Because some people park money at the bank for several months or years, the interest rates earned on different types of accounts are an important variable. A popular activity in the blogosphere is comparing various online bank accounts to determine which ones are currently offering the highest rates. Ken, over at www.bankdealsblog. com, has dedicated the majority of his site to locating these deals, but discusses other offers and sign-up bonuses as well. Many consumers chase these deals by moving their money around to whichever bank is currently offering the best rate. I've found that some of these opportunities are valuable, but reading the fine print concerning fees and minimum balance requirements is crucial.

For all that the aforementioned factors are objective and can be used to figure out which bank is *technically* the best, the bottom line is how you *feel* as the consumer. Corporate bank chains would drown out most local banks if customers thought without emotion and focused only on features. Some people don't like the often rude and sterile chain banking experience in which small account holders take a backseat to wealthy clients and businesses. Many of those small banks still know your name and value your business.

What Makes a Bank *Bad*?

In my experience, what makes or breaks a bank is the quality of service coming from its employees. This ties into the preceding paragraph but becomes a bigger issue when the service aspect is negative, as opposed to "corporate neutral," as I like to call it. A friend of mine recently closed his checking account, only to discover that it had not been properly closed. As a result, an accidental charge of $25 was debited from his empty account to pay for his monthly Internet service. Because the account had a zero balance, the $25 charge triggered a $30 overdraft fee. What should have been a closed account quickly turned into a $55 negative balance, a major argument with the bank teller, a possible credit issue, and a giant headache. There are lots of ways these problems can happen. Upon finding what you believe to be a reputable bank, try to develop a relationship with at least a few tellers and customer service representatives. This way, you have somebody who may actually care when you have a problem. I've found that these little personal relationships can go a long way.

When you open an account, whether checking, savings, or money market, you must ask about the minimum balance requirements. Whereas the offer of a 5 percent interest rate for a savings account may lure you into a bank, the offer will lose most of its appeal when you discover it only applies to each dollar over $15,000. For every dollar below, you may be getting only 1 percent interest. This was my first experience with a savings account, and I felt it was unfair. I shopped around until I found a bank that would pay me more than 1 percent, even if I was depositing only a few thousand dollars. In some cases, there will be no minimum balance requirement, but until your account reaches a certain level, a $20 or $30 monthly service charge may apply. This is more or less the same thing as getting a worse interest rate since the fee will erase the marginal benefit of the higher interest rate. Again, you can usually compare these requirements online to find the bank that best meets your needs. A few web sites are listed at the end of this chapter that have already compiled the majority of this research for you.

Similar to how low fees can give banks an edge, high fees can drive away customers. The first time you get smacked with a $30 fee for an overdrawn check, or pay $25 because your father wired you money, it may leave a bad taste in your mouth. Regardless of how much money you have, nobody likes to feel taken advantage of. Ask for a fee schedule and zero in on the fees that apply to you.

 Note: Most banks understand that fees can alienate clients. If you get hit with a fee for the first time, ask the bank to remove it as a courtesy. Many banks will do this for you once, and if they don't, it may be a signal to move your money.

More Banking Tips

For some people, finding a bank with an international presence may be an important factor. If you travel abroad often, and your bank has multiple branches overseas, this could improve the efficiency of money transfers, currency conversion, and borrowing funds for real estate and business transactions.

I've also noticed recently many banks incorporating credit card services into their product lineup. This is smart business. It conveniently allows the consumer to view credit card and personal banking information on the same screen. It also allows the user to process transactions between accounts. This concept of integrating bank services has become more widespread as banks look to improve branding and customer loyalty. Why not consolidate the majority of your banking needs in the same place if it's advantageous to do so?

One of the more important things to remember is that different banks work with different personalities. If you run your own business and desire interaction between your accounts, a more corporate culture will probably appeal to you. However, if you're retired and usually stick to simple and predictable transactions, the smaller bank may be preferred. Take a walk around your current bank and try to observe the culture. That may sound silly, but give it a try. Once you're comfortable with a bank, create a friendly relationship with the various tellers and service representatives. You may be surprised how much this goodwill can improve your banking experience.

For More Information

When it comes to almost any type of personal banking, especially interest rates and lending questions, www.bankrate.com is the authority. Bankrate.com's motto—"Comprehensive. Objective. Free"—is right on target about what the site provides. I'll mention this web site throughout the book in chapters where it is useful.

We've already mentioned www.bankdealsblog.com, which is my favorite reference for comparing bank deals, but several other personal finance bloggers are covering this topic as well. Flexo, over at www.consumerismcommentary.com, keeps fairly steady updates on competitive bank offers as they are publicized. You can also visit www.mymoneyblog.com for some banking comparisons. In fact, this is an excellent stop for any reader who is new to the financial blogosphere. Certain features on this blog (such as the net worth tracker) will allow the reader to feel embedded in the financial journey of the blogger. This can help the reader make better sense of the posts and see how the blogger includes reader input in his or her financial life.

Web Hot Spots

www.bankrate.com

www.bankdealsblog.com

www.consumerismcommentary.com

www.mymoneyblog.com

CHAPTER

2

What Are Personal Financial Statements, and Why Do I Need Them?

Once you become serious about building your net worth, a certain curiosity or awareness will surface with regard to your personal finances. You may start to scrutinize your spending a bit more, cutting back on frivolous purchases and focusing on smart investment choices. But how do you track financial progress? What framework should you use to determine where you are financially and where you are going?

Among the first lessons one learns in financial planning is how to *quantify goals*. If clients tell you they "want to be rich," make them define that statement. For some people $1 million will be enough. For others, $10 million is the target. Often goals aren't in the form of money, and my job becomes quantifying them. After we define goals, we can figure out a way to get there. It makes sense, doesn't it?

The two financial statements I tend to utilize in my office are the balance sheet and the cash flow analysis. I also like something called the statement of personal objectives, which ties these worksheets together in a psychologically healthy sort of way. We'll get around to that toward the end of the chapter.

You may envision these sheets as not applicable to you or overly burdensome, but everybody should have a method of tracking their net worth. It's easy to do and will better illustrate the areas of your financial life that you can improve upon. Let me show you how to create personal financial statements.

The Balance Sheet

The balance sheet, shown in Figure 2.1, is a snapshot of your financial condition as of a certain date. The three broad categories on a balance sheet are assets, liabilities, and net worth. The balance sheet should be updated at least once a year; otherwise, tracking the factors that influence your net worth will become more difficult. I often encourage clients to update balance sheets quarterly, because revisiting one's financial situation more frequently will lead to taking more actions. The following items typically appear on a personal balance sheet:

- *Liquid assets.* For our purposes, liquid assets will be cash on hand along with other accounts that are easily accessible. The most common assets in this category are cash, checking accounts, and savings accounts. You may also have a certificate of deposit (CD), or a money market account that you can access with a check or debit card.
- *Investments and retirement accounts.* There may be some overlap between liquid assets and your investment or retirement accounts. This is not a problem, as the overall goal is to have a general understanding of what your assets are and where they are held. Be sure to include individual retirement accounts (IRAs), vested balances of retirement plans at work, and the cash value of life insurance policies. You may also have stock certificates, savings bonds, or some other form of redeemable capital.
- *Physical assets.* These are assets that can generally be converted to cash when and if necessary. We try not to include less expensive personal belongings, which may have a small market or are difficult to value. Major physical assets include: homes, buildings, other physical structures, automobiles, artwork, jewelry, and boats. On the balance sheet, we list the total value of each physical asset rather than giving the value less what we owe in mortgages or loans; we'll have a place in our liabilities for mortgage balances and outstanding loans. The ultimate

ASSETS

	Current Value ($)
Personal Bank Accounts (checking, savings, money market)	
Certificates of Deposit (CDs)	
Personal Income Investments: Bonds, Bond Mutual Funds	
Personal Stocks and Stock Mutual Funds	
Real Estate Investments	
Business Interests (proprietorships, partnerships, company stock)	
Retirement Plan Investments	
Individual Retirement Accounts (IRAs)	
401(k) or 403(b) Plan(s)	
Keogh Plan	
SEP or SIMPLE Plan	
Profit Sharing Plan	
Pension Plan	
Market Value of Home(s)	
Cash Value of Life Insurance	
Personal Property (jewelry, collectibles, cars, furniture)	
Miscellaneous (trust interests, inheritances)	
Total Assets:	

LIABILITIES

Mortgages	
Car Loans	
Credit Cards	
Student Loans	
Other Loans	
Outstanding Bills/Obligations	
Total Liabilities:	

NET WORTH
(Subtract Liabilities from Assets)

ASSETS:	
LIABILITIES:	
YOUR NET WORTH:	

Figure 2.1 How Much Are You Worth?

15

goal of the balance sheet is to increase the value of assets over both long and short periods of time.

- *Liabilities.* The balances we owe are our liabilities. They can be current liabilities such as a credit card balances or longer-term debts such as student loan payments. Common liabilities include: mortgage or home equity balances, rent payments, automobile loans, medical bills, credit card balances, and business loans. You may also have education expenses, such as a private loan, and perhaps a computer or camera that you financed at your local electronics store. Most people aim to reduce liabilities over time, especially as a ratio of assets.

- *Net worth.* Assets – Liabilities = Net Worth. This is the bottom line. If you own $100,000 between equity in your home, an investment portfolio, and a checking account, but you owe $10,000 on your credit card and $5,000 to a friend, your net worth would be $85,000 ($100,000 – $10,000 – $5,000 = $85,000). If you proceed to pay $10,000 the following year toward your home and pay off the $5,000 debt to your friend, you would then be worth $100,000. As you can see, this isn't rocket science. Personal finances can often be improved simply by looking at them squarely to realize what shortfalls may exist. The final net worth value is what you reference to monitor your financial progress. It is hoped that this number goes up, not down, and increases steadily throughout your life.

The Cash Flow Analysis

The cash flow analysis, commonly referred to as a budget, is a key component to improving your net worth statement. (See Figure 2.2.) You need to figure out the smartest way to allocate your money each month so that your assets are increasing, your liabilities are decreasing, and you're able to pay your monthly expenses. All of this should happen without feeling too much pressure about money.

Cash flow analysis can reveal some interesting facts about your lifestyle. You may find out that, on average, you spend $500 per month on your dog, or perhaps that you lost $5,000 on Vegas trips that could have been socked into retirement accounts. Most important, it should reveal if your lifestyle is too expensive, it is impractical, or (one hopes) it is well within your budget. Here are the components of a monthly cash flow analysis.

INCOME   Current Value ($)

Salary and Earned Income

Child Support and Alimony

Pension

Social Security

Dividends, Interest, and Capital Gains

Business Interests (proprietorships, partnerships, company stock)

Other Income Sources

Total Income:

EXPENSES

Rent/Mortgage Payment

Car Payment

Credit Card Balances

Student Loans

Other Loans

Taxes (Fed/State/City + Real Estate)

Insurance (home, auto, life, etc.)

Savings/Investments (401(k), 403(b), Savings, Investments, etc.)

Food Expenses (dining out and groceries)

Utilities

Clothing

Vacations

Other Habits and Hobbies on Which You Spend Cash:

Total Expenses:

CASH FLOW

(Subtract Expenses from Income)

TOTAL MONTHLY INCOME:

TOTAL MONTHLY EXPENSES:

MONTHLY NET CASH FLOW:

Figure 2.2 Monthly Cash Flow Analysis

Income

In the income section of the worksheet you want to include all your sources of income for a given month. This step might be difficult if you don't get paid a regular salary. Working on commission or running a small business might require the use of assumptions. Whereas this may decrease the accuracy of the budget, it's still a good framework to utilize when analyzing your spending. In terms of taxes, I prefer to use gross income figures (including taxes) and then subtract tax dollars as an expense in the liabilities section.

Be sure to include all of your income sources for the month in this section. Being honest about your income will make the financial planning process easier, even if requires admitting to financially supportive parents or a less than moral side business. C'mon now, we're all trying to make a living. Typical income sources include salary, wages, interest income, royalties, real estate, and gifts.

Expenses

Trying to itemize expenses is always an interesting process. Most people tally up the numbers and it appears that no financial shortfall could possibly exist. Then we speak a bit more, and all the "Oh, yes" and "Whoops, forgot about that" purchases come out. Eventually it all makes its way onto the paper. We'll delve more into the budgeting process in Chapter 3.

The largest expenses generally stem from housing, transportation, and food. Yes, the average person spends several hundred (if not several thousand) dollars per month on food. This section should also include taxes, out-of-pocket health care costs, utilities, vacations, and debt payments. It's generally easier to include your credit card bill as a monthly debt payment rather than trying to itemize all of the $10 and $20 expenses that we have but have trouble remembering.

Some people add in their own sections to the cash flow worksheet. Perhaps separate columns for "desired expenses" and "actual expenses" could help illustrate your spending patterns. Remember, the overall goal of this worksheet is to improve your own awareness regarding spending and savings.

For some people, mostly those in their 50s and 60s, cutting spending is discussed, even embraced, but with only a grain of seriousness. I've given lectures on budgeting and observed a certain look of disinterest or skepticism regarding cutting back on spending. The only answer for these people may be to increase their current income. If working harder doesn't accomplish this, often an investment portfolio can be designed such that most of the holdings are geared toward providing income.

The Statement of Personal Objectives

I feel more like a psychologist than a financial adviser when I start talking about how to achieve personal objectives, but good financial practices are often tied to having personal objectives. When I first started working with financial statements, I believed that making progress on the balance sheet should be the primary concern; if your net worth is improving over most quarters, I'm doing my job properly. It then occurred to me that my own advice would require a deeper objective than just improvement.

So now I request one or two personal goals that can be reached each quarter when updating net worth. A goal doesn't have to be something unrealistic, or even overly ambitious. In fact, an objective is often to continue doing something that is productive. Common financial planning goals may include increasing your contribution to a retirement plan over some period of time or speaking to a relative about establishing a college savings plan.

Part of the benefit of having a statement of personal objectives is to elicit the feeling one gets upon meeting a goal. This form of self-validation and achievement often lends itself to better practices in other areas of life as well. Remember, money is emotional. This is something I will talk more about later on.

The Bottom Line

Feel free to copy the corresponding worksheets in this chapter and use them in your financial life. I will reference these sheets throughout the book, as they are crucial in the planning process. I hope that with time you can add more rows within your asset categories to account for your growing portfolio of real estate, valuable business assets, and increasing number of investment accounts.

For More Information

Tracking net worth is a very popular activity in the blogosphere. As a dedicated reader and writer of blogs, I can admit it's quite addictive to observe individual financial behavior. I don't display my own personal finances online because I'm a bit more of a private person, but I appreciate the lessons learned from those who do. Each blogger has different financial priorities and certainly differing opinions about what represents a good or bad financial decision. Two must-read bloggers who track their net worth online are Flexo over at www.consumerismcommentary.com and the anonymous author of www.myfinancialjourney.com. You'll notice when visiting Consumerism Commentary that Flexo has both a comprehensive cash flow analysis and a net worth statement that is updated monthly. It really is quite impressive.

Another fun visit is www.financialbabysteps.blogspot.com. This blog tracks the financial musings of a baby and the steps she (and her parents) take to make her financially secure for life. Needless to say, I have this blog on my favorites list. I would also recommend visits to http://allfinancialmatters.com and www.bargaineering.com/articles. These are excellent personal finance blogs that offer advice on budgeting and include discussions about keeping personal financial statements. There are actually numerous blogs that could apply to this chapter. To find more, check out the blogrolls posted on any of the sites mentioned.

 Tip: A blogroll refers to a list of blogs that the author reads. The collection of links can be used to reference blogs with similar content, to highlight recently updated blogs, or simply to promote the work of friends.

Web Hot Spots

www.consumerismcommentary.com

www.myfinancialjourney.com

www.financialbabysteps.blogspot.com

http://allfinancialmatters.com

www.bargaineering.com/articles

CHAPTER

3

Can a Budget Really Help Me?

A basic budget is an important building block for other good financial practices. Once your cash flow is under control, you'll have a much easier time making decisions about future expenses, savings, and investments. If you can grasp the concept that sacrificing a few items today will allow you to buy more items later, you'll have a better chance at affording luxuries such as houses, cars, vacations, and college educations for your children. I had a difficult time conveying this concept to my brother, who believes that money is better enjoyed as a younger consumer in the world and becomes an item of necessity rather than pleasure as one gets older. I think what he's referring to are life events such as marriage, children, housing, and education—which are expensive and typically require a large percentage of your after-tax funds.

I agree with him in one respect: that money has more shock effect when spent on items that pass quickly, such as vacations and meals. However, he may be overlooking a crucial link: responsible spending on the not-so-fun things such as mortgages and retirement savings is directly related to one's ability to spend more later on. There are objective realities (the classic examples being death and taxes) that we need to plan around. If we are to lead fruitful lives, understanding the impact of today's spending will help us, rather than hurt us, down the road.

This chapter covers the budgeting basics that I consider to be important and integrates the financial journey of a hypothetical friend of mine, Jay. He is a single male who lives in Chicago and is having trouble keeping to a budget. I'll also point out some popular blogs that give fascinating and extremely detailed discourse on individual budgeting tactics.

What Are the Basics of a Budget?

The three necessities of life that tend to cost the most are housing, transportation, and food.* Think about how much time you spend in your home, getting from place to place, or eating.

Time can be a funny concept in that it puts into perspective just how similar the activities of most human beings are. In fact, the percentages of money spent on these three items are nearly identical for both low-income and wealthy families, the differences being the size of the home, the newness of the cars, and the variety of meals. As a rule of thumb, spending approximately one-third of net income on housing is a responsible figure. This means if you earn $40,000 but your take-home pay (after taxes) is $30,000, you should not be spending more than $850 per month on either your rent or your mortgage payment. Keep in mind that each person's situation is different, and many factors could alter this percentage (higher or lower).

The next third of your after-tax pay should cover food and transportation. While I tend to think this percentage could be lower, food is obviously a popular and often expensive industry. It makes economic sense, because people love to eat and generally don't kick up too much of a fuss about paying food bills.

Transportation has a similar story: A majority of people could drive economy cars that utilize alternative energy sources, but choose not to. We drive sport utility vehicles that cost $50 or more to fill up at the gas tank. The economic explanation for this is that we don't feel the pressing need or collective desire yet to radically alter the way we transport ourselves. While these subjects warrant discussions of their own, the point is that much of what could be comfort money is spent to cover the sky-high costs of eating and getting around.

Let's apply this to Jay, our financial planning example. Jay is a true city personality—a computer programmer, single, with a very active lifestyle. I chose him as an example because his after-tax, disposable income is around $2,500 per month, fairly close to median income statistics in the United States. I believe his situation typifies in

---

*U.S. Department of Labor, Bureau of Labor Statistics' Consumer Expenditure Survey 2004.

many ways the sort of budgeting mistakes many people tend to make. The rent on Jay's studio apartment is $1,000 per month. Although this is above the $850 maximum per month I would have recommended, he partially compensates for it by not keeping a car in the city.

Jay's apartment, including his cable and energy bills, costs $1,200 per month. He spends a total of $14,400 each year, or 48 percent of his disposable income, on the apartment. Jay could easily lower that number to $10,000 by either getting a roommate or taking a place further from the center of town. But besides the fact that Jay likes where he lives, he insists on keeping the apartment because transportation costs would become too high if he moved further away from his job.

Food is an important expense for Jay as well; he eats only organic and tends to shop at stores like Whole Foods and Wild Oats. However, he doesn't eat out at restaurants very often, which offsets the expense of locating organic foods. He estimates he spends $4,800 per year or 16 percent of disposable income on food.

Transportation is the third largest expense at 8 percent of his disposable income, or another $2,400 per year. It would seem that most of the big-ticket items are out of the way at this point. However, Jay not only spends his disposable income each year, but he saves nothing and is starting to develop credit card balances (it's not *actually* a syndrome). His other hobbies include taking an annual trip to Florida with friends, buying music online, and playing poker. Jay says there are probably a lot of expenses he is forgetting such as birthday gifts, haircuts, gym membership, and the like, which push him over his spending limits. Our estimate is that despite having $30,000 in disposable income left after taxes, Jay spends $31,000 per year and saves nothing. Saving, he insists, is something he'll start thinking about in his 30s.

How Can I Save More?

We will get to advice for Jay shortly, but first, I'm going to reveal something to those of you who claim that you *can't* save. The secret is:

Here's how.

If you get paid on the first of the month, have $100 (or some amount that looks feasible but not strenuous)

Treat saving like a monthly bill.

systematically withdrawn from your bank account and directed into a savings vehicle. Depending on your time frame and risk tolerance, this could be something simple and liquid, such as a savings account, or it could be some combination of stocks and bonds.

Also, if you have a retirement plan at work, you should consider utilizing this vehicle before some other type of account. The reason is that retirement plans usually have tax benefits that make them desirable for longer-term savings. You should start this habit of automatic saving as early as possible and never stop. Granted, you may start earning larger sums of money, in which case $1,000 per month would be better suited for you. Regardless of the amount, saving money should be as high a priority as any bill is. If it's not, cut your HBO and start with that extra $10 each month.

Next, ditch high-priced coffee and start making it at home. Quitting coffee alone could save you $100,000. Does that figure sound crazy? Take a look at Table 3.1, which examines the opportunity cost of spending $3.00 a day. If coffee is a bad example for you, substitute some other habit you could cut back on: cigarettes, buying lunch, or excessive dry cleaning.

This chart could be used to illustrate other financial planning concepts, such as the time value of money and the effects of compounding. For now, we're concerned only with opportunity cost: what we forgo when we spend $3.00 instead of putting it into the bank.

Now let's look at some changes that I think could benefit Jay's financial situation:

Table 3.1   The Opportunity Cost of Spending

Year	Cost per Cup	Cost per Year (3% Inflation)	Total Paid All Years	If Money Had Been Saved Instead at 7% per Year
1	$3.00	$1,095.00	$1,095.00	$1,172.00
2	3.09	1,127.85	2,222.85	2,427.00
3	3.18	1,161.69	3,384.54	3,768.28
5	3.37	1,232.43	5,814.00	6,739.14
10	4.03	1,428.72	12,553.00	15,554.34
20	5.42	1,920.07	29,423.00	45,059.82
30	7.28	2,580.27	52,095.00	103,101.54

Jay will cap food store runs at $50 per week ($16 less than his current average). This would save approximately $832 per year, which could be invested. We made this decision upon a further discussion in which Jay revealed that he tends to try out new products but could probably buy just as much food even at $50 per week.

He is starting to use a debit card or cash rather than a credit card for expenses. Studies show that people who spend mostly cash tend to be more frugal, while active credit card users tend to overspend. Jay was a classic credit card user who paid back less than his full balance at the end of each month. This practice gradually leads to higher credit card balances.

Jay will investigate retirement plans that are available to him at work. He will begin contributing the minimum to the company 401(k) plan, a move that will reduce his taxable income and create savings.

Jay would like to establish a vacation fund to avoid using his credit card for his annual trip to Florida. He will begin saving $75 each month by having it automatically deducted from his checking account and deposited into an interest-bearing account.

He will discuss with his employer opportunities to earn more money.

Do I Have to Keep a Budget Even If I Earn a Lot of Money?

Budgets aren't just for those who are struggling with money. In fact, budgets often increase in importance as your finances grow and become more difficult to track—just ask Mike Tyson and Michael Jackson. Each of these once-superrich celebrities has been in the news for having major financial troubles. Maybe I'm missing something here, but that just doesn't seem right. The self-proclaimed King of Pop was earning over $30 million per year during parts of the 1980s when his popularity was peaking, and the former heavyweight champion earned $48 million in year 2000 *alone*. Disregarding their recently degraded reputations, you'd think each of them should have more money than they ever could possibly need. In fact, when interviewed on *The Big Idea with Donny Deutsch* in 2006, Tyson explained that he didn't have adequate financial guidance and suggested that a paid professional could have made a big difference. The point is that analyzing cash flow might have helped Tyson gain some perspective on his irresponsible spending.

Another group of people who tend to have trouble staying on top of their finances are those who work in sales or other commission-based jobs. Some of these people may earn $20,000 one month, take three months off, and then earn $20,000 again. It can be very tricky to make a longer-term spending plan with this type of erratic earnings pattern. However, the three steps are the same:

1. Write down your expenses.
2. Analyze what you could be cutting back on.
3. Be sure to save a little something each month.

For More Information

Budgeting is a very popular topic in the blogosphere. It's not easy for me to isolate the best budgeting blogs out there because I read a good 30 or so that are worthy of mention. That being said, some may be a bit more user-friendly for new blog readers than others.

We'll start with http://frugalforlife.blogspot.com. Dawn, the author, believes that frugality is a way of life. Rather than the traditional view of frugality as a sacrifice of some sort, she feels it can be both fun and fulfilling. Visiting her blog will shed a whole new light on saving money.

I'm also a fan of http://budgetingbabe.blogspot.com. This Chicago-based site, run by a young lady named Nicole, is dedicated to "all the young, working women who want to spend like Carrie in a Jimmy Choo store but have a budget closer to Roseanne." This is a fun blog that is filled with valuable information.

Savvy Saver (http://savvysaver.blogspot.com) never fails to introduce me to new and innovative ways to save money. The author is committed to sharing smart decisions regarding how to live within one's means and build a higher net worth in the process.

The Money Blog Network (www.moneyblognetwork.com) is an aggregator service that compiles blogs from top personal finance bloggers. We will find that the authors who comprise the Money Blog Network will be useful in more than one chapter of this book. One particular contributor, known as "FMF," writes www.freemoneyfinance.com, an extremely comprehensive blog that is filled with tips on everything from budgeting to improving your career and understanding your taxes.

Finally, I have bookmarked a really great site that can teach you how to maximize what you can purchase with a dollar. It can be found at www.stretcher.com. This incredible resource will help you save money in ways you haven't even thought of. Visit the topic library at the bottom of the home page for the long list of articles.

Web Hot Spots

http://frugalforlife.blogspot.com
http://budgetingbabe.blogspot.com
http://savvysaver.blogspot.com
www.moneyblognetwork.com
www.freemoneyfinance.com
www.stretcher.com

4

Are Credit Cards My Enemy?

Americans tend to have mixed feelings about credit cards. They appreciate having easy access to funds, but largely resent the tendency created by credit cards to overspend. Credit card issuers exacerbate the problem by pushing the use of credit on consumers and tangling a web of fees and interest charges along the way.

However, having access to credit is an extremely important part of today's financial world and helps to validate the consumer. It allows one to conveniently buy things located anywhere, and creates the ability to make reservations for services such as car rentals, hotels, and restaurants. I would say that credit cards are already an item of necessity rather than luxury. It's difficult to make it through a year as an active person without having some sort of access to credit. The convenient record-keeping and surveillance aspects of using credit over cash have made it an appealing choice for consumers and vendors alike.

As this dependence on credit cards continues to spread, it's important that you understand the benefits and drawbacks to credit cards, why they cost consumers so much money, and how you can avoid falling into credit card traps.

What Are the Benefits of Plastic?

Before I embark on a rant about why credit cards are dangerous, I'd like to emphasize that responsible usage can provide you with all types of rewards—and I don't just mean free flights and gift cards.

One of the most important benefits is purchase protection. When you buy something for cash and it gets damaged, it's very unlikely it can be returned, even if you believe it wasn't your fault. When you pay with a credit card, though, you can challenge a transaction if a legitimate problem exists. Let's say a vendor sells you a damaged product and you can prove it. You very well may be able to challenge that purchase because you paid for it with a credit card. Purchase protection is a huge advantage provided by credit cards.

Establishing credit history is also an important benefit. By acting responsibly with your access to credit, you help shape the way future lenders will view your eligibility for loans. Credit analysis is tricky in that you must exhibit good financial habits when you don't need a loan to establish good credit for when you *do* need one. If a bank is considering giving you a loan and it sees you rarely make a late payment or go over your spending limit, it will be more likely to extend credit to you.

Finally, as we mentioned before, credit cards are great for organized record keeping. Since all the activity can be viewed electronically, you can track what you buy, when it was purchased, how often payments are made, and so on from the convenience of any computer.

What Are the Dangers of Plastic?

For me, and I'm sure for many others, spending a hundred dollars on the credit card is a very easy thing to do. I also find that it takes on a different meaning than pulling a crisp hundred out of my wallet. The simplicity of spending on cards, whether $50 or $500, encourages increased frequency and larger amounts of spending.

A good analogy is playing casino games with chips rather than cash. The reason casinos require the use of chips is to induce a game-like atmosphere where players focus on building up chips rather than thinking about the potential saving or spending opportunities for the money on the table. Perhaps we should put a disclaimer on credit card receipts that would be similar to the one on a pack of cigarettes: "Please be aware that you are about to spent $260. Please take out 13 $20 bills, look at them, and think this through. Are you positive you can afford to do this?" Maybe that would curb some spending.

Besides running up high balances, other drawbacks related to credit card spending include the interest charges and fees. When we leave unpaid balances on credit cards, finance charges build up. The longer we wait to pay down those balances, the more we'll pay in interest. For many consumers, the balance builds up quicker than anticipated and can take months or even years to be paid down. At points like this, when you stare at your Italian leather sofa and just wish it could be returned for something less expensive, you start to understand why credit cards are so evil. The $2,000 price of a sofa quickly becomes a cost of $2,200 as your interest charges accrue and you get hit with a fee for paying a day late. Situations like this need to be either avoided altogether or carefully managed.

When a new client comes in looking to invest money, I tend ask about credit card balances in the same discussion. Because the interest rates on many of these cards exceed the sort of investment return a person with a moderate risk tolerance could handle, it often makes the most sense to pay down the credit card balances before starting an investment plan.

 Tip: The Consumer Credit Protection Act was the first piece of federal legislation specifically designed to protect consumers. Title I of the Act, known as Truth in Lending, requires increased disclosure about the terms and costs of credit transactions. While I'd speculate that credit providers didn't love this piece of legislation, I don't think it has made a shred of difference in the care taken by consumers prior to obtaining and using credit. These companies don't need to hide information about their terms and costs. They can spell out how they get paid in plain English and remain confident that the use of credit cards will either remain steady or increase.

What's an APR?

Some of the financial jargon thrown around by credit card companies is not fully understood by the spending public. For example, interest charges are often quoted as annual percentage rate (APR) on statements and other mail you receive from credit card companies. When you first apply for a card, many promotions offer an *introductory rate* APR. This percentage rate is generally good for only the promotional period, typically six months or a year, and then reverts back to your standard APR tables for purchases, balance transfers, and cash advances.

You might not notice when and if rate changes occur if you don't review your statement in detail. Many consumers look only at their total balance due each month and then figure out how much they feel like paying. The better thing to do is go over your statement for a few minutes each month, make sure the purchases look familiar, and the interest charges (if any) make sense based on stated APRs. Other terms besides APRs can change at the end of promotional periods. One should really try to take note of when those changes may happen.

Also, an advertised APR for a credit card may appear to be low—say 12 percent. However, that percentage can often vary depending on a number of factors. First, if you transfer over a balance from a different credit card, the APR is usually higher. If you take out a cash advance, this often triggers the highest APR. And while you may not track the different interest rates you pay on purchases, balance transfers, and cash advances, the credit card company does. Ask for a breakdown of your interest rate charges if you get confused.

Finance charges will also vary based on the calculation methods used to determine how much you owe. One part of that equation will be the APR. A lower rate will be better in almost all circumstances.

Another big factor is whether new purchases are being included in your outstanding balance. If you sometimes carry a balance, you should look for a card that does not include new purchases. This will allow you a period of time, usually until the end of your billing cycle, in which you can pay off new purchases without incurring any finance charges for them. Also, the computation of your balance, from which interest charges are based, can be calculated in different ways.

The two most common methods are *average daily balance* and *adjusted balance*. The adjusted balance method is calculated by simply adding up your purchases and other charges each billing cycle and subtracting payments and other credits. The average daily balance method differs from this in that your average balance is recalculated *daily* based on new purchases, payments, and other activity. When using this method, one needs to take note of the time between when charges are made and when they are paid down.

While I tend to prefer the adjusted balance method, this should really not be the determining factor when evaluating credit cards. I would encourage you to focus more on making large, on-time payments and maintaining a reasonable APR.

What About Fees?

For starters, I'm not a big fan of the annual fee. If you are paying it, there should be a good reason to do so. This could be a low APR, a card with special privileges, or a card issued to someone with less than perfect credit. In the latter example, the issuing organization is taking on more risk and the annual fee serves to compensate it for that additional risk.

If your card doesn't fall into any of those categories, ask your provider to remove the annual fee. In the world of credit, if you don't ask questions, you probably won't get answers.

The two most common penalty fees on credit cards are for paying late and for going over the spending limit. When dealing with responsible consumers, the credit card company will often waive a first late fee or over-the-limit fee. Don't be shy; just call up and ask nicely for them to remove it. If they really appreciate your business, they'll work with you.

How Can I Raise My Line of Credit?

Your credit limits are based on how responsible you are with your cards. If you regularly charge up your credit cards near their spending limits, you will probably not see your credit lines increase very often. This is because a credit card company will view being close to the limit as a sign that you aren't able to pay down the balance. Keeping a balance that is 10 percent or less of your available credit is generally considered within the responsible range of most lenders.

You may also be able to get an increase simply by calling up and asking. I tried this once out of sheer curiosity, and it worked. They'll generally check to see what your average balance is and how frequently you pay on time.

I'd like to share an interesting story regarding spending limits that illustrates how credit card companies look to make money. My original impression was that paying my balance in full each month would lead to the most rapid increases in my credit lines. I learned this isn't always the case because not as much money is generated off consumers who never carry balances. I spent a period of my life carrying balances from month to month amounting to about 10 percent of my available credit. I noticed that my credit line increased faster when I left a small balance than when I paid the balance in full. My guess is that by showing I was able to occasionally pay the card in full, but choosing to carry a balance, I became the ideal consumer to profit from. I certainly don't recommend trying that—it just gives you some perspective on the logic that goes into decisions about credit lines.

What About the Cards I Use Now?

A great way to start making changes in your financial life is evaluating the cards you currently use and getting new ones if your current ones aren't fitting your needs. Before you apply for a new card or take advantage of a balance transfer offer, consider which credit card features appeal the most to you. For instance, if you are like the many other Americans who don't pay their balance in full each month, try to get a credit card with low interest rates. However, if you charge everything to your card but always pay the balance in full, you might care less about interest rates but want a good rewards program.

I have a friend who buys everything on his credit card, pays his balance in full each month, and at the end of each year cashes in his points for a plane ticket to Hawaii. Try to evaluate your spending so you can find benefits that truly coincide with your card usage. Card Web (www.cardweb.com) is a great site for locating the credit card that is right for you. It breaks down credit card offers into specific categories such as business, student, and prepaid, among others, which can help you find the one that best fits your needs. The site also has helpful payment calculators you can use to estimate how long it will take to pay down your balance, a question and answer section, and access to free newsletters.

If you don't feel like applying for a new card, you can try negotiating the APR on your current cards. Because credit is a competitive industry and issuing companies understand that you have the choice of either canceling your account or transferring it to a different credit provider, you constantly maintain some degree of bargaining power. If you call up and demand a lower interest rate, the company is put to a decision of either granting your wish or rejecting your request. Many consumers actually do not follow through with threats of closing their cards because they have anxiety about making changes. If this sounds familiar, try to overcome fears of financial change and make decisions that increase your bottom line.

If you are having financial problems, credit providers actually will listen to you as well. If they reasonably believe that someone might not be capable of making payments, they might lower the interest rates and impart some financial planning advice. I find it highly unlikely that they actually want you to be debt free, but they'll be mildly accommodating if a reasonable possibility exists that you will otherwise have to stop making payments altogether.

So, from now on, don't immediately throw away those credit card offers. Some of them may actually offer great terms, including a zero percent interest rate for the first year, if you stay within your spending limits and never pay late. You could even jump from card to card each year taking advantage of deals like this. I know people who do it. Be careful not to become too obsessed with capitalizing on credit card deals as this may impact your credit score or become an organizational issue.

The best thing to do is find a card or two that work for your individual situation and make you happy. As a general piece of advice, try not to carry more cards than you can handle. I find that two or three are often plenty and usually recommend against taking on retail cards. These are the kind that give you 10 percent off when you apply for them at the cash register. They tend to have very high interest rates, so don't apply for one unless you pay your balances in full each month and spend often with that particular retailer.

For More Information

Bankrate.com (www.bankrate.com) is a personal favorite of mine, both for credit card topics and other areas of personal finance. Besides the background information you'll find in the credit card section, you can also read its credit card blog, Plastic Rap. To find it quickly, use the search box on the upper right side of the home page.

A blog that has truly stepped up as one of the best personal finance blogs in the past year is www.thesimpledollar.com. The target audience of this blog is 20- and 30-somethings who are facing unique personal finance challenges compared to earlier generations. Trent, the owner, went through a financial meltdown because he believed he should be following the same spending and debt models of his parents. However, he discovered that this model no longer works. The blog tells of his experiences starting over and shares what he learned.

Finally, I would recommend a visit to www.fivecentnickel.com. This is a classic personal finance blog, widely recognized as one of the blogosphere's best. I've chosen to drop that link in this chapter because I've read and learned from some of its credit card posts. However, after you get through some of those, you'll want to surf around the site for other interesting entries as well.

Web Hot Spots

www.cardweb.com

www.bankrate.com

www.thesimpledollar.com

www.fivecentnickel.com

5

Am I Scared of My Credit Score?

Credit scores remind me of the SAT exam. In theory, they represent one's aptitude for managing credit. In reality, they give lenders a very rough idea of one's habits when it comes to handling money. While the SAT is a major determinant of which undergraduate colleges will accept an applicant, it's hardly a measure of who the ideal candidates for each school should be.

Unlike the SAT, a credit score will follow most people around for the rest of their lives. Checking your score regularly and understanding its underlying components will undoubtedly improve your financial life. The sooner you take an interest, the better. If there's one financial mistake that I've seen all too often, it's a lack of credit score investigation prior to applying for a loan. This type of error affects people of all income levels and is avoidable with some basic planning. Let's make sure you're a smart consumer and use your credit score to your advantage rather than to your detriment.

Which Factors Affect My Score?

The most important factor in compiling a credit score is payment history. It should be fairly logical that lenders would want to check your past behavior regarding financial obligations before lending you money. This includes payments on your home, car, credit card, cell phone, and any other line of credit you may have open. Late payments on major loans such as mortgages are going to be viewed more seriously than late payments on a cell phone or gym membership. The amount of lateness, whether 30, 60, or 90 days, will make a difference as well. You may only get a slap on the wrist for paying your credit card 30 days late. However, skipping over the car payment for three months will stick out like a sore thumb to potential lenders evaluating your score.

This section of the report also includes the number of delinquent accounts you have, the length of your delinquency, and the amount of money in question. The worst type of delinquency is a bill that hasn't been paid at all and remains in collection. This often happens because consumers are confident that they do not owe money to somebody who claims they do. Whereas chucking the bill into the garbage may be the morally justifiable thing to do, you must think in terms of your future. If possible, clearing up any past controversies before they end up on your credit report is the better action to take. It may be possible to have those items removed from your report later on, but it's a lot more difficult to handle after the fact. It's very frustrating to clear up an old cell phone debt years after the discrepancy took place. You may not remember exactly what happened, and having a precise recollection may be the only chance you have of getting the item removed. The bottom line: Deal with credit discrepancies when they arise.

I was interested to learn that not all organizations report to credit agencies. Some companies have in-house collection departments that call you up looking for money. Others outsource to third party collection agencies that will harass you with phone calls until you either pay the bill or reach some form of settlement. These people tend to use less-than-admirable methods when seeking payments. You should ask these collection agents if they report to a credit agency before you start arguing or reach a decision about whether to pay the bill.

Another factor that could affect your score is the ratio of balances to available credit for your open accounts. Lenders like it when you are readily capable of obtaining credit but handle such a privilege responsibly. Often they are looking to see that you don't utilize the majority of credit that is available to you. Credit cards are a great example of this. You might have a credit line of $10,000 but keep a balance of only $500. The scoring agencies love to see such discipline with your available credit balance. Keeping your card 90 percent maxed out implies that you can't afford to pay down your balance. Interestingly, lots of people who can afford to pay off their balances each month choose not to for a variety of reasons.

Tip: It's almost always a better idea to pay off credit card debt rather than using the money for other purposes. This includes investing, where your rate of return will most often not match the interest rates on your cards.

I'd like to clear up one last item about this section of the credit report before moving on. Consumers do not get automatically penalized for borrowing large sums of money. The amount you borrow isn't the most important question. The score is reflecting *how you handle* the open lines of credit that you have.

The length of time that one has maintained credit lines will also be reflected on the score. This element of payment history deals with your long-term consistency. Ultimately, this can help solidify a high score. A consumer who makes 10 payments on time is developing a good pattern. Once that consumer has made 100 payments on time, the score may start reflecting this sort of consistency. As a result, more lenders will be willing to negotiate with this type of consumer. The likelihood that they will default on future payments is viewed as lower after those 100 payments have been made.

A consumer could also be penalized for opening up too many lines of credit in a short period of time. I once argued with a credit scoring agency on behalf of a client who was very responsible and couldn't figure out why his score was hovering in the 600s. We learned that he had opened up four lines of credit within a three-month period. Apparently, in the seemingly mystical algorithm that compiles one's credit score, this was considered an irresponsible thing to do, even though it was coincidental. One must remember that these scores aren't a concrete science and keep a tab on them.

If you are a younger consumer, you may benefit greatly from having access to another person's established line of credit. Twice in my life I've noticed credit scores in the high 700s that belonged to people in their 20s. I found this hard to believe, given how short their credit history was. The reason in both cases was that somebody else had given them access (usually through a credit card) to a line of credit with a positive history of payments going back 20 years or more. Naturally, this same logic can come back to bite you. If you hold a line of credit from a card user with a spotty history, it can negatively affect your credit score. Ideally, an excellent credit history is something you should be able to share with others whom you trust and respect.

What Is Considered a Good Score?

If we use Equifax, one of the largest consumer credit agencies, as our example, the score range is between 300 and 850. To be perfectly honest, I've never met somebody with a score of 850. I wouldn't even be so sure it's possible to maintain a score like that. These numbers can change based on the day of the month or even the hour of the day they are requested. A good score, which should make you a fairly competitive candidate for a loan, is in the high 600s. Above 700 is excellent, and whether you're a 740 or a 770 you will likely secure a very competitive rate when borrowing money.

Other factors besides your credit score will influence your ability to borrow money. You may get lucky and apply for a loan at a time when the mortgage business is very slow. If this is the case, you may secure a competitive rate even if you have a lower score. If you are applying for a loan when interest rates in the economy are high, you could have an 800 and still find yourself paying a higher interest rate than your neighbor with a 600 who applied for a mortgage a year ago. This scenario happened in the early 1980s when Americans were grappling with sky-high interest rates. The point is to understand the importance of your credit score but realize that it's viewed in context with other factors.

The three major credit reporting agencies—Equifax, Experian, and TransUnion—may all have different scores for you. Whereas all three *should* have similar information, I've seen scores vary quite widely from one agency to the next. This is why prospective lenders will often pull all three to gain a broad perspective.

What Rights Do I Have as a Consumer?

Many consumers don't realize that they have certain rights established under federal legislation known as the Fair Credit Reporting Act (FCRA). One of these rights is to receive a free copy of your credit report each year. In practice, it's easy to get the credit report for free, but the score usually costs a few bucks. The official web site to help you obtain your free credit report is www.annualcreditreport. com. Most of the other sites will try to talk you into a fee-based credit management package, which provides a current copy of your score and offers a variety of credit management tools. This may actually be useful if you're looking to boost your score and keep a tab on changes.

The FCRA also gives you the right to dispute information that you may find to be inaccurate on your report. The best part about this clause is that the credit agencies must launch the investigation on your behalf. After a consumer disputes an item, a progress report is mailed out within a few weeks with updated information on the investigation. If the findings are in your favor, the credit agency must correct the information on your report within 30 days. In practice, all of the procedures mentioned require a little bit of nagging, hold time, and frustration. This is why it's wise to investigate your credit a good six to nine months before you apply for a major line of credit.

The FCRA is actually a very interesting piece of legislation to read through. It prohibits most of the unusual tactics formerly used by lenders when credit assessment was a more vague science. Lenders used to visit the neighborhoods of potential borrowers in search of information that could help them better make a decision about the applicants' credibility. Catching a quick conversation or behavior, they figured, could provide some useful knowledge to the lender. I'm certainly glad this practice is specifically prohibited now, as it resembles stalking.

What I've Learned about Credit Scores

We've talked about some of the factors that help derive your score, so this is a good place to provide a few of my own realizations about the credit services industry. For the record, it's not one of my favorites.

Sometimes lenders have strict rules about scores. For example, a 680 might qualify you for a quarter percentage point discount on your home loan. However, if you have a 676, you won't qualify. These four points could amount to thousands of dollars over the length of your loan. This is one reason to check in with your score at least once a year.

Mistakes happen all the time. I've pulled my own credit score and seen errors that I couldn't even make sense of. They were resolved once it was clear that some organization had reported an item in error. Don't ignore an error because you're intimidated by it. Credit agencies will investigate the error on your behalf if you simply call them up and ask. Always ask questions if something doesn't look right.

Credit scoring is a business, not a government program. My advice is partially knowledge I've gained from reading through credit reports and another part common sense. The reason so much ambiguity surrounds this industry is that profit is involved. Keeping a certain level of confusion about the components of a score and how to fix it allows the scoring business to evolve and those involved to make money.

Neither your income nor your net worth is reflected in a credit score. This number is not about rewarding the rich and punishing the poor. It's about evaluating financial behavior. Don't think that just because you earn several hundred thousand dollars that you'll get a competitive mortgage rate. It might help you obtain the mortgage initially, but it won't help your interest rate.

For More Information

BrokenCredit (www.brokencredit.com) is a great blog that I recently stumbled upon. It was created to assist the public with information about credit repair and responsible mortgage lending. All of the information on the site is free, and most of the authors are mortgage and real estate industry professionals. However, there are also individuals on the site who share their own experiences.

Emily Davidson, moderator of www.creditbloggers.com, is a former credit expert from TransUnion. This site brings together numerous experts to share answers to credit, loan, debt, and identity theft questions.

Besides these two blogs, you'll notice that most of the active personal finance bloggers mentioned throughout the book have credit-related posts. They vary widely from tips on improving your score to discussion forums that share the experiences of consumers.

If you want to search through a larger volume of background information, visit the personal finance sections of www.smartmoney.com or http://moneycentral.msn.com. These references will be good for credit questions in addition to most personal finance or investing issues.

Web Hot Spots

www.annualcreditreport.com

www.brokencredit.com

www.creditbloggers.com

www.smartmoney.com

http://moneycentral.msn.com

PART

II

BUILDING WEALTH REQUIRES PLANNING

6

What Is the Role of a Financial Adviser?

The question of whether or not to work with a financial adviser is a personal one. For some people, dealing with financial issues is unpleasant and requires a great degree of undesired discipline. Are you nodding your head? Well, I hope this book can get you more excited about personal finance. If you're one who tends to avoid financial issues completely, the important question will be *how* to choose the best adviser, rather than *whether* to work with one.

Other people embrace financial decisions on their own, whether placing investments, purchasing real estate, or creating and monitoring a budget. My findings have been that many of those who are most eager to work with advisers are actually fairly knowledgeable about financial issues. They confer with professionals to reinforce ideas and seek second opinions about what they may already know. This is a smart strategy. I always enjoy working with people who embrace their finances. For example, some people have a really good feel for the investing process, but they don't understand much about life insurance. Others may understand insurance but they find estate planning to be overwhelming. A professor once told me that anybody wise enough to handle all aspects of personal finance on their own should probably be in the business of advising others. This wasn't always the case, but financial issues have become so complex and convoluted that even experts must meet up to refresh themselves from time to time.

This chapter gets into some of the reasons one might work with a financial adviser. I'll also touch upon how to choose an adviser and how they get paid. Professional compensation seems to be all the rage lately in magazines, journals, and even the blogosphere. I think a more widespread understanding of compensation models (and the fact that financial planning doesn't have to cost an arm and a leg) could lead more people to work with advisers.

Giving a few examples of financial planning scenarios should help you better understand the value provided by a good adviser. It may also shed some light on financial planning issues that are important to you. As a side note, I tend to use the terms *adviser* and *planner* interchangeably. Although these two terms often refer to people in the same profession, some would say that a "planner" may have a greater focus on financial processes, while an "adviser" is either a stockbroker or somebody who deals with planning issues as well.

- *Traditional financial planning.* Take for example a married couple, gainfully employed, and living in a home with two children. This is a great case for financial planning because of how many planning questions a family like this may deal with. The three biggest hurdles—in order or expense—will be saving for retirement, putting money away for college educations, and possibly supporting aging parents. The not-so-beautiful part about these three issues is that they all fall in sequence, usually over a course of 10 or 20 years. The husband and wife probably also want their family to live in decent style, dress well, and take the occasional vacation. Most important, they need enough liquidity to comfortably cover all the necessities. This couple should start by filling out financial statements to lay out a plan going forward. Priorities will be discussed, often enlightening a spouse in the process. The adviser will highlight possible savings vehicles to meet each goal. Working out potential tax issues in advance can be a blessing as well.
- *Goal planners.* This financial planning scenario frequently involves people in their mid-30s who are earning a decent wage and starting to focus in on their net worth. Perhaps you want $1 million saved up by age 59, not including the value

of your home. This amount, you've concluded, combined with a pension, will provide adequate retirement income. We will deal with these priorities in two phases: accumulation and dispersion of assets. The process here is mathematical in nature, involving a timing schedule and target amounts to save each month. Risk tolerance and investment options will be important as well.

- *Speculative clients.* There are plenty of people who are less concerned with the exact age when they can stop working and are more focused on taking risks now to make money. Let's be realistic. Not all 30-year-olds are socking their disposable incomes into tax-deferred accounts. It would give me personal joy if they did, but thinking strictly in terms of financial safety is boring to some investors. I've learned firsthand that being realistic with clients is one important way to obtain their trust. Plus, being speculative may not be as short-sighted or immature as some advisers make it out to be. We've all heard the phrase "risk/ return trade-off," and many of those who take calculated risks are living in better style as a result. These clients may obtain an adviser to help them pinpoint the risks that are specific to a potential investment. They may also need the adviser because they can't utilize certain investing strategies or products without one. Or they may simply want to consult about a list of stocks they are considering investing in. Perhaps the adviser is better qualified to do research and can be resourceful in the analysis process. On the topic of investing resources, you should find plenty of free resources mentioned throughout this book.

Perhaps at least one of these scenarios sounds familiar to you. Beyond these examples, a good financial planner can help with many other financial processes. One of the more important ones in my experience is clarifying your current situation. There are traditional ways of doing this, such as putting together financial statements you can use to track your progress. This is something I do in my practice, and most people can start benefiting from such financial statements immediately. Then, there are methods that are specific to each individual client.

This is where the planning process gets interesting. To effectively implement a change in someone's financial behavior will often require a certain level of honesty and trust between a client and an adviser.

Money is an emotional part of life, and often some hand-holding goes a long way. If you allow your adviser to understand your quirks, the planning process becomes much easier.

What Can a Financial Adviser Do for Me?

One observation I made when I first entered the business was that much of financial planning is common sense. If you actively pursue certain behaviors, such as saving and budgeting, you may find they aren't overly confusing and they simply boil down to discipline. I went on to learn that the pursuit of such discipline is often the hardest part. For this reason, the coaching aspect of financial planning is very important, even for clients who have a comprehensive understanding of financial issues.

A good adviser can also teach you about investment vehicles that exist for different forms of savings. For example, 529 plans are designed to help save for higher education expenses.* This type of plan is named after Section 529 of the Internal Revenue Service (IRS) tax code and allows for both tax-free growth and tax-free withdrawal of funds if they are used for higher education expenses. This provides a nice incentive for using a 529 plan rather than accumulating funds elsewhere. An investor might simply not be aware of this savings vehicle without consulting an adviser. You can quickly learn what the potential opportunities and drawbacks are and become a more knowledgeable saver.

Other examples of beneficial vehicles for tax-deferred savings include individual retirement accounts (IRAs), 401(k)s, and 403(b)s. A common mistake made by investors is saving for retirement outside of retirement plans. If you have a long-term savings goal and you can utilize a vehicle that will reduce your taxes and allow your money to grow free of capital gains tax, this would be a good thing to know about. It especially irks me when a person passes up an employer

---

*As with other investments, there are generally fees and expenses associated with participation in a 529 savings plan. In addition, there are no guarantees regarding the performance of the underlying investments. The tax implications of a 529 plan should be discussed with your legal and/or tax advisers because they can vary significantly from state to state. Most states offer their own plans that are similar to 529 plans, which may provide advantages and benefits exclusively for their residents and taxpayers.

match (free money), which often comes as a benefit from a company. However, not everyone understands these different vehicles, so they simply ignore them and utilize a savings account instead. Your planner should help you understand what the potential benefits of these vehicles may be. Then it's up to you whether to embrace them.

Planning for a specific goal is another popular area for advisers. This process goes hand in hand with creating and maintaining a budget. If you need $30,000 for a down payment on a house and you have $10,000 today plus your future earnings potential, you can usually figure out with decent accuracy how much you need to save today to meet your goal. Perhaps $2,000 saved annually for seven years plus accrued interest will be sufficient. If you divide this cost monthly, this additional $20,000 in savings will run you less than $175 per month. That isn't quite as scary, is it?

Some advisers have a specialty. By homing in on a specific market, such as high-net-worth clients, the adviser can become familiar with the issues dealt with by their target demographic. Some financial planning firms have multiple advisers, each with a different area of expertise, so that the office has a huge amount of collective knowledge. Common specialties include insurance, investments, retirement, estate planning, and taxes. In the next chapter, we discuss some of the different types of financial professionals and how they contribute to the planning process.

I'd like to briefly talk about the misconception that financial advisers are just for the wealthy. Nowadays, personal finance issues can be as complicated for the middle class as they are for the rich. Many middle-class people have a tax adviser, financial planner, and stockbroker, all working on separate issues. If you don't work with any of these professionals and you have the knowledge to do it on your own, that's great. However, most people don't realize that often a simple flat fee can buy them a financial plan that will improve their understanding of their current financial situation and map out a plan for the future. Try to keep an open mind, and find a planner who will sit down with you to develop a plan for all the areas you may need help in.

How Do I Choose the Right Adviser?

Some planners obviously won't mesh with you, and that's okay. A common misunderstanding is that just any financial adviser will be able to answer all your questions and explain concepts in a way that you can understand. You must find an adviser who works well with your personality. A good relationship with an adviser could last many years, and feeling comfortable should be a top priority. A desire to work with somebody similar to you in age is something I find is pretty common as well.

There are a few standard questions a prospective client can ask to better understand the planner's business. The first is what, if any, are the planner's professional affiliations? An affiliation with the Financial Planning Association (www.fpanet.org) or the National Association of Personal Financial Advisors (www.napfa.org) is obviously a good thing. It can't hurt to have an adviser who keeps up-to-date on industry news and has a handle on new industry policies and ideas. You might also ask how long the office has been open, the type of client the planner caters to, and whether the firm has been involved in any regulatory or disciplinary action. This might seem like more information than you're entitled to ask for, but it's not. Disclosure is extremely important in the financial services industry, and you have every right to know about the disciplinary history of a firm with which you may do business. You'll also want to ask about fees and commissions, which we'll get to in a moment.

Advisers can be found in a number of ways. My experience has been that most people find them through referrals. If someone has a good adviser who has done well by them, they will speak about it to their friends and co-workers. You could also find a new adviser online, through organizations such as the Financial Planning Association. Finally, there may be a local financial planning office near where you live. Most advisers (not all, but most) will offer a free consultation when you first come in. This will allow you to assess whether you're comfortable working with this person. It'll also give you a chance to ask the aforementioned questions and see if you like the responses.

How Do Financial Advisers Get Paid?

In the past few years, many professionals in the advising field have switched their compensation model from commissions to fees. The logic for such a switch is very clear. Once an adviser has earned a commission from the sale of an investment product, that adviser has little incentive to service the account. In fact, the real incentive is to go out and seek more business to earn new commissions by selling more products. If you earn a living on commissions and don't actively seek out new clients, your income is going to suffer as a result.

If an adviser earns a fee, especially if that fee is ongoing, the incentive is toward continued service of the account. There are generally two ways a fee-only financial adviser can get paid. The first is a perpetual fee based on assets under management. A 1.5 percent annual fee for a $100,000 account earns the adviser $1,500 per year. If the account doubles in size, the fee doubles as well. If the account loses half its value, the fee gets cut in half. The other method is to receive a flat fee, either hourly or per financial service provided. This is generally the cheapest way to obtain financial planning if you can find somebody talented who is willing to be compensated in this way. Perhaps you will pay $500 in exchange for a financial plan that you can implement on your own.

I find that fees based on assets under management are becoming increasingly common, as they allow the professional to make a decent living. This compensation arrangement is mutually beneficial for the client and the adviser, which makes for a healthy relationship between the two. That being said, there are plenty of situations in which paying a commission will ultimately be cheaper for the client. This is a fact that many people overlook simply because of the gray cloud forming over commissions. Fees that continue for the life of the account can certainly add up over the years. A commission can be paid up front and be done with.

If you're genuinely concerned about paying the least amount of money for financial services, ask the adviser which way is cheaper, commissions or fees. Don't be shy—it's something advisers understand they must discuss. Have them explain all the compensation details so you can make the decision that is right for you.

For More Information

My own blog (www.russellbailyn.com/weblog) is a popular resource for financial planning. I think part of the reason for its success is the fact that I work in the industry but retain my ability to explain financial concepts in an everyday sort of way. Some advisers speak in such complicated jargon that their clients nod their heads but don't really have a clue what's going on. I believe a client should be involved in the process the whole way through. I aim to make personal finance exciting, rather than boring or confusing.

As I mentioned earlier, some people rely strictly on books, magazines, and articles to navigate the world of personal finance on their own. This is actually the intended audience of many personal finance bloggers. "FMF," the author of www.freemoneyfinance.com, is a passionate do-it-yourself investor. His blog is dedicated to helping people grow their net worth through money-saving strategies, self-study, and sound advice.

The Financial Planning Association (www.fpanet.org) has a search tool that allows you to find a Certified Financial Planner (CFP) in your area. The CFP designation, as we'll discuss in Chapter 20, is the ultimate credential for a financial planner. The search tool even allows you to find planners based on specialty areas of practice, something we talked about earlier. It's a great stop to make if you want to take a peek at the world of financial planning.

In terms of a more traditional web site that may be good for reference, I like http://money.cnn.com. This portal has interesting articles on financial planning topics.

Web Hot Spots

www.fpanet.org

www.napfa.org

www.russellbailyn.com/weblog

www.freemoneyfinance.com

http://money.cnn.com

CHAPTER

7

How Does the Financial Planning Process Work?

We've discussed the role of a financial adviser or planner, the questions one might ask a prospective adviser, and how he or she typically gets compensated. But how does the science of financial planning work? What makes it effective? We'll find that it's actually rather formulaic, and often involves more discipline than it does complicated decision making.

Naturally, it would be impossible to stick precisely to a formula, because life throws us curveballs that can change our plans in an instant. For example, winning the lottery would increase your budget dramatically—but hey, we'll worry about that one when it happens. A good planner will be able to integrate good changes and bad into your financial plan and keep the process moving forward regardless. I've found that clients who understand the planning process and dedicate themselves to it often benefit greatly as a result.

What Are the Six Steps of the Financial Planning Process?

There are six steps associated with the financial planning process, according to the International Organization for Standardization (www .iso.org). Let's delve into each one to better understand the scope of each objective. These are the same steps learned by candidates sitting for the Certified Financial Planner (CFP) designation, which is a popular credential found within the planning profession. There are also six areas of preparation that are commonly associated with comprehensive financial planning. We'll discuss those as well.

Step 1: Initial Consultation with an Adviser

It's a simple fact: Some people work better together than others do. This can be the result of a match in personalities or an ability to relate to someone for reasons including age, gender, lifestyle, and priorities. I am one of the younger advisers at my own firm and have noticed this firsthand. A certain comfort level and, subsequently, a better business relationship result from good cooperation. Being sure about your financial planner is important because this relationship will often last many years, and a healthy balance of tempers can lend itself to better financial progress.

As I mentioned in the preceding chapter, initial consultations are often free. The prospective client is coming in to meet the new adviser, present his or her situation, and talk about financial goals. Meanwhile, the adviser listens carefully, shares his or her own perspective about financial planning, and explains the method of compensation. The decision to work together is mutual. While I think that an initial consultation should be free, some advisers do not agree. Perhaps if you get slapped with a bill on a first visit it will signal you to look elsewhere.

Step 2: Gather Client Data

Once you've defined the scope of your relationship, it's time to get into more specific detail about your finances. You may have visited a financial planner thinking your primary objective is to improve your return on investment. After a brief conversation, your planner discovers other issues that should be priorities as well—perhaps refinancing a mortgage or funding a child's education. The planner tries to view the big picture regarding your financial life by gathering both quantitative and qualitative information. The distinction here is crucial. Quantitative data are any hard facts that an adviser can gather from a client. Qualitative information explores wants, needs, and desires.

Tip: The ability to reveal qualitative data, such as your deepest concerns, to your adviser may be the trick to discerning and implementing the right financial plan for you.

In terms of what all this information is, quantitative data refers to income sources, tax returns, credit card receipts, mortgage stubs, and investment statements. Qualitative data includes risk tolerance, lifestyle decisions, family dynamics, employment expectations, social sensitivities, and political affiliations. Gathering the right data is crucial in that it allows the planner to organize your information and make sense of it.

Step 3: Analyze and Evaluate Client Financial Status

This is the step where financial planners can demonstrate the added value of their services. If a client doesn't already track cash flow and net worth with financial statements, this would be the time to put them together. That not only helps the client view a snapshot of his or her financial life, but it can be utilized by the adviser to track progress as well. As I mentioned earlier, financial statements are the benchmark from which to work when it comes to monitoring your progress. The two financial statements that we're most concerned about are the net worth statement and the cash flow analysis.

The evaluation process will often reveal a lot about a person. Viewing credit card transactions might expose a tendency to overspend at certain times of the year or a recurring expense that could easily be eliminated. A good planner will bring in factors you may not have considered that affect your financial situation. These may include current economic conditions, knowledge of financial products, and ideas about how to minimize taxes. The adviser can crunch this information together to develop the best possible plan for your needs.

Step 4: Present Recommendations to the Client

This stage is when the planner presents his or her ideas to the client. In practice, this often occurs on the second or third visit. Most recommendations are going to excite clients because they symbolize positive financial changes on the horizon. Naturally, certain recommendations might be unacceptable or be challenged. This could happen for any number of reasons and is perfectly normal. One client of mine rejected a stock recommendation because she didn't like the reputation of the CEO, regardless of the company's stellar performance. Sound crazy? We've all got our quirks, and we've also seen the sudden downfalls of CEOs along with their companies (Enron, Tyco, etc.). Another client indicated a certain willingness to tolerate risk that I quickly learned was bogus. Once he started calling up daily to check the value of his stock portfolio, it became clear that he wasn't able to handle the volatility associated with the stock market.

A planner should pay close attention to the reaction of a client to recommendations. This may give some further indication of personal preferences that weren't picked up at a prior meeting.

Step 5: Implement and Monitor the Financial Plan

If a client's primary objective is to invest $100,000 with growth as a top priority, now is the time to put that money to work. You've presumably already discussed various investment options with the client, as well as how the fee schedule works. Now it's time for the adviser to execute. It often helps to answer in advance any questions that the adviser knows from experience typically surface at this point. For example, I like to teach people how to read an investment statement before they actually receive one in the mail. I also like to explain the fact, especially when it comes to investments, that disclosure is mandatory. If they start getting lots of mail that makes little sense, it's because recent law necessitates that the client receive notice of all activity that affects the account, whether or not the client cares to read it.

The monitoring process is all about updating financial statements to test the value of the plan. If assets are moving up and liabilities seem to be under control, progress is being made. If you've never practiced financial planning before, you'll most likely embrace the monitoring process. It's good to check in with your finances every now and then. I recommend doing it each quarter, although I've found that in practice most people are willing to do it only once per year.

Step 6: Review and Revise the Plan

As we have indicated, life tends to throw us curveballs. Perhaps you saved up $50,000 for the college education of your child, who then was awarded a full scholarship. This would be one of those positive examples of when a financial plan needs some amending. Perhaps the majority of those funds can now be applied toward retirement, which will in turn reduce the monthly contribution you have been dedicating toward your retirement plan. This may improve your cash flow and ease up your month-to-month expenses.

Of course, the opposite is possible as well. If your elderly parents suddenly need a chunk of money and you're willing to help them out, your financial plan may require some tweaking. Perhaps your darling rich sister won't cough up any money to help, and no other way to mitigate these costs exists. Pushing back your retirement age by one year may cure the problem instantly. However, this may not be something you're willing to sacrifice. If not, cutting back on a vacation fund, temporarily reducing your savings, or considering ways to earn a higher income may be necessary. It usually turns out that life hands us several obstacles at once, with some being better than others. The good news about your child receiving a scholarship could wash out the bad news about helping your elderly parents. Because financial plans aren't set in stone, we'll continue to revisit the plan and revise it as necessary.

What Topics Are Covered by Financial Planning?

There are six topics typically covered by the financial planning process. There are multiple subcategories that exist as well, but most of them fall within the basic six categories. One useful aspect of working with a financial adviser is that they often have connections with other helpful people. If they can't answer a question, someone they know can. Relationships are normally in place to cover any potential shortage of knowledge that may be recognized by the firm.

1. *The financial planning process.* These are the six steps outlined earlier. Having a client understand these steps is regarded by many planners as necessary before moving on to other topics. If someone isn't willing to embrace their financial lives properly, it's often not worth pursuing any further course of action. Once the desire is there and financial statements have been created, the planner and client can move on to the following topics.
2. *Insurance (risk management).* The reason this often appears high on the priority list is that without properly managing

one's risk exposure, the financial plan could fall through entirely. We study risk in four ways: reduction, assumption, avoidance, and transfer. Risk transfer, generally to an insurance company, is an extremely important concept to understand. The policies you own can protect you from a variety of potentially hazardous situations. We'll visit this again in Chapter 24.

3. *Investments.* Investing will often be at the center of a financial plan. I've found that prior to starting an investment program clients should understand why they are investing and what various investment options may be available to them. The process of investing differs for each individual and is something to be discussed in context with a financial plan.

4. *Taxes.* Planning for taxes is something we all have in common. Those who avoid thinking or dealing with taxes until April rolls around aren't planning properly. Not only can planning in advance ease your tax burden, it can ease your mind as well. Taxes integrate themselves into all aspects of the financial planning process, from investing and insurance to retirement and estate planning. Often a financial planner will consult with various tax professionals when implementing a certain tax strategy. Tax decisions can get quite sticky, depending on the complexity of the client's situation.

5. *Retirement planning.* This is perhaps my favorite financial planning topic. It often requires a lot of information to arrive at the most suitable strategy. You must first determine personal factors, such as an age to retire, an amount to retire with, and an estimate of what your various income sources may be. Retirement plans such as the 401(k), 403(b), and IRA are popular savings vehicles that allow for certain tax benefits if the rules of the plan are strictly followed.

6. *Estate planning.* I've found that people often associate estate planning with the end of life and therefore avoid it like the plague. Having a discussion about how to ease the transfer of your assets and figure out who should get them is not always the most pleasant topic. However, avoiding estate issues for too long can end in a giant headache for your family and friends. It could even result in your money ending up in places it was never intended to go. An example of that would be forgetting to update the beneficiary on a life insurance

policy. Certain estate planning issues can be integrated into retirement and investment decisions, but most often estate planning must be dealt with on its own.

Each of these categories could, by itself, be a specialty topic that a financial planner focuses on. In order to become a Certified Financial Planner, one must have passed individual exams that touch on each of the six topics prior to sitting for the comprehensive examination. As we'll discuss in Chapter 20, there are financial credentials that exist for people wishing to specialize in one specific area of financial planning. For example, the Chartered Life Underwriter (CLU) is a specialty insurance designation, and the Qualified Plan Financial Consultant (QPFC) is specific to the retirement arena.

For More Information

The information in this chapter covers the six steps in the financial planning process and the topics generally covered throughout that process. While following the formula is a smart approach to planning, one should expect to revamp their strategy to accommodate unforeseen changes.

The Internet is a great place to read up on various aspects of the financial planning process. I visit the web site of the Certified Financial Planner Board of Standards (www.cfp.net) at least a few times per year. It's a good stop to make to obtain information from an authoritative voice in the financial planning industry. Sometimes reading an authority's web site such as this will give you some deeper insight, which is what you are looking for.

About.com (www.about.com) and Forbes.com (www.forbes.com) have very comprehensive personal finance libraries. You can reference these sites for basic planning information or to read current news that may be affecting the industry. I refer back to these sites throughout the book because I find them extremely useful. I also bookmarked a neat little consumer resource called "Building Wealth," which was established by the Federal Reserve Bank of Dallas. It's a beginner's guide to financial responsibility and presents information in an organized fashion. It can be found at www.dallasfed.org/ca/wealth.

Not many blogs are dedicated strictly to financial planning. My own blog, www.russellbailyn.com/weblog, fits this criterion, and I'm confident there will be more blogs specializing in financial planning in the next few years. We've already seen a pattern emerge in which blogging is being recognized as a useful business tool. The issue has gotten a decent amount of press, and I have a feeling this pattern will continue in 2007 and 2008.

One other adviser who writes an excellent blog is Scott Dauenhauer. His blog, "the Meridian," can be found at http://themeridian.blogspot.com. He covers financial planning, investment management, and how world events may affect your portfolio. We'll visit Scott's blog again in Chapter 11.

Web Hot Spots

www.cfp.net

www.about.com

www.forbes.com

www.dallasfed.org/ca/wealth

www.russellbailyn.com/weblog

http://themeridian.blogspot.com

CHAPTER

Why Is Money Emotional?

Upon reading all of this advice about personal finance and investing, you might think you should be following a defined set of rules. For example, in Chapter 7 we laid out six precise steps to execute a financial plan. We also discussed the six topics which broadly comprise the world of personal finance. It's no surprise that individual investors and experts often mistakenly see investing and financial planning as exact sciences. Regardless of advice you receive and literature you read about what you *should* do with money, it won't change one perennial truth: Financial decisions are guided by emotions.

I'm not by any means suggesting that financial decisions should be as emotional as they are. In fact, many experts are doing you a favor when they advise that you establish an investment plan and stick to it as closely as possible. Even so, financial transactions remain in the same boat as buying a home or even choosing a spouse: your own feelings will matter as much as (or more than) what is technically the right or wrong thing to do. Plenty of literature has been written about this concept—much of it teaching how investors can overcome emotional issues and get better financial results. We talk in this chapter about how emotions come into play with your investment decisions and in the personal finance arena as well.

What Is Emotional Investing?

Emotional investing refers to letting your own feelings mix into the investment process. It can best be explained in the context of behavioral finance, which tries to understand the relationships between psychology and investing to figure out anomalies such as the technology bubble, which popped in 2000. Behavioral finance also helps explain certain attitudes toward risk, as well as reactions to sudden gains and losses of money. Observing the behavior of people who win a lottery or receive an inheritance is revealing. Certain people will blow through the money while others won't change their lifestyle at all, regardless of how much money they come into. Some have speculated that a careful understanding of behavioral finance could be used to profit from the stock market. This counters the efficient markets hypothesis (EMH), which states that stock prices already factor in all known information about the company. True believers in EMH probably wouldn't try their hands at stock picking because they don't believe individuals can, over an extended period of time, outperform the broader market indexes.

To give a clear illustration of how emotion can dominate the stock market, let's talk about what happened with the NASDAQ Composite index between 1999 and 2002. At the beginning of this cycle, investors were dedicating a tremendous amount of cash flow toward technology stocks, most of which were brand-new and had very short revenue histories. Nonetheless, investors bid the prices of many tech stocks up to unthinkable levels. After reality checked in, the NASDAQ dropped precipitously until the end of 2002, giving up gains going back as far as 1996. It was an ugly scene.

What explanation could there be for the NASDAQ losing the majority of its value between 2000 and 2003? It wasn't rocket science, but rather a pure emotional roller coaster. In 2002, even though tech stock valuations had come down to reasonable, if not inexpensive, levels, nobody was buying. In fact, most people were still selling. Yet, when the prices were sky-high a few years earlier, everyone was rushing into the market. This is indeed the opposite of how to make money. The best strategy, if you had an effective way of doing so, would be to buy stocks when prices are low and sell them when prices are high. Yet many, if not most, investors buy stocks after they have already become expensive and sell them long after they've gone into decline.

In my own practice, I've noticed another clear example of emotions dominating investing. It occurs with clients who leave a job and have large amounts of company stock in their retirement plans. We usually sit down to have the obvious conversation about diversification. "Hi, Mr. Doe. It sure looks risky that you keep 80 percent of your retirement assets in the stock of your former employer. Why don't you exchange some for a basket of different stocks?" I then hear something along the lines of: "Well, the stock has done nicely since I started working. Do you think it's so bad if I keep most of it?" The decision is ultimately up to the client, but I always do my best to explain why keeping the bulk of one's retirement funds in a single stock, especially when nearing retirement, can be a dangerous thing to do. Unfortunately, an emotional attachment can easily form when clients spend the majority of their working years with the same employer. It could be viewed as abandonment or betrayal to sell that stock for some other companies that they have little to no attachment toward. That feeling could become even worse if you sold your company stock and it subsequently began to rally.

There are actually many ways emotional investors can fall behind the market indexes. For example, some people, regardless of performance numbers, don't like to buy value-oriented investments. They find them boring and unlikely to return a large profit in a short period of time. I suppose in some way the latter criticism is valid, but not in any way an intelligent investor should be thinking.

Take Warren Buffett, an investment legend. For all that I respect him, I'm going to discount his enormous success for a moment to make a point. Buffett's strategy is fairly simple, and his requirements for placing investments haven't changed much throughout his career. Unlike some other portfolio managers, Buffett didn't jump onto the technology bandwagon in the late 1990s when everyone was trying to get rich quick. Buffett simply doesn't buy into companies without a consistent history of earnings, management, or some other area in which he can find value. So, while some people may have laughed at him during 1999 when they were making money hand over fist, most of them crashed and burned while Buffett rode through the bubble as if it never even happened. His secret is simple: He didn't fall into emotional investment patterns that even the most disciplined investors fell for.

There are countless examples of these investment errors. Most of them result from investors abandoning their principles for an attempt to make a quick dollar.

Investment Products for Emotional Investors

Selling investment products is a business. If we accept this as truth, it's logical to believe many products are created with the needs of consumers in mind. For example, index funds try to mirror the performance of a specific index, such as the Dow Jones Industrial Average or the S&P 500 index.* Part of the reason these funds have such a popular following among do-it-yourself investors is that they provide direct and inexpensive exposure to various market indexes. It removes the emotional burden of seeking out performance through stocks and actively managed funds. This would be a smart product to utilize if you find yourself chasing performance but haven't been able to get the return on investment you're looking for. As I tell clients, focus on costs and diversification. These are aspects of investing that you can control. Don't waste time analyzing the markets yourself unless either you are a Chartered Financial Analyst (CFA) or you get some major enjoyment from playing with stocks. Trying to pick individual stocks will probably reduce your return while costing you more in the process.

We speak in Chapter 21 about investment products offered by insurance companies. As we'll discuss, hands-on investors will often pass up annuity-style products in hopes of creating lower-cost alternatives on their own. However, the many people who aren't oriented toward personal finance may be drawn to certain features provided by the insurance companies, such as a guarantee of the principal amount invested. In fact, these features are marketed in very direct ways toward people who will retire without pensions and will rely mostly on personal savings. The insurance industry is probably not as worked up as the rest of us about the looming decrease in government benefits. A reduction in Social Security or pension funds could be an opportunity for the insurance industry to continue to innovate with its investment products.

I also find the popularity of asset allocation funds to be an interesting phenomenon. These funds, if you haven't heard of them, try to accomplish the goals of asset allocation and diversification all by themselves. The investor has no need to buy multiple funds, investigate holdings, analyze stock-to-bond ratios, and so forth. This cookie-cutter product just needs to know your age and can work around that. Talk about a product geared toward emotional investors!

---

*You may not invest directly in an index. Actual performance may vary based on fees, expenses, and other factors.

This one avoids scenarios such as buying high and selling low, simply through ownership of one fund. This product has a very specific appeal to passive investors who want to accomplish certain financial planning objectives without having to do all the legwork themselves. Asset allocation funds are also popular for education savings programs in which the money is invested more aggressively while the child is young and slowly transitions to a more conservative allocation as the child approaches college age.

Certain people, generally those with a lot of money, tend to avoid asset allocation funds because they can afford to take on more risk. Remember, some investors don't like the idea of a portfolio consisting entirely of bonds.

Other Financial Issues That Are Emotional

Investing isn't the only financial process that can be diverted by emotion. Spending money is a fascinating example as well—one that can really throw off a financial plan. I was in high school the first time I heard the expression "retail therapy," which basically refers to a desire to spend money after a bad day or tragic event. Who wouldn't be in a better mood after buying a new suit or handbag? Unfortunately, too many people shop to feel better and then regret it when the credit card bill comes around.

Spending money is not just a reaction to stress. It can commonly be a reaction to happiness or boredom as well. I've noticed that my clients' spending increases around holidays and other times when the family comes to town. These are occasions for buying gifts and hosting visitors. Often spending increases because a trip to the mall or visit to a nice restaurant is more fun with the family. While this is all very logical, sometimes money is just acting as a medium for entertainment or thrill that could be accomplished in other, less expensive ways. For example, in my own family we tend to play board games when we all get together. Scrabble, Monopoly, and Scattergories are our personal favorites. This is not to suggest we never shop or see a movie; however, we derive a lot of pleasure from time spent together playing games. This activity arouses plenty of emotion and helps avoid end-of-the-month financial blues. That's a quick piece of advice that I hope saves you thousands.

Saving can be emotionally equivalent to spending, but tapping different feelings at different times. People often don't make saving a priority unless they understand what they are saving for. If I tell clients they will need $750,000 more to retire comfortably, they'll probably listen and put some money away, but usually not with strong motivation. It's not often a client will get excited about saving a lump sum of money for a vague future purpose, especially when it necessitates a change in lifestyle. However, saving for a down payment on a home or for a vacation is a much more exciting concept. People must be able to make positive emotional connections with the item they are saving for. This is precisely why quantifying your goals with as much detail as possible is so incredibly important in the financial planning process. Perhaps once retirement has been equated with a beachfront condominium in Miami, you'll ditch the idea of buying new shoes every week and sock that money into high-yield savings instead.

The concept of paying down a mortgage might explain why home equity represents a large chunk of retirement savings for many Americans. Buying a home and paying down a mortgage allows people to buy something and save up money at the same time. The home is both a savings vehicle and something you can live in. Psychologically, it may be a more pleasant way to save than through stocks and bonds.

What Should I Make of All This?

When it comes to investing, the question of how to handle emotion is a bit complicated. Investment experts are correct when they say that most investment decisions should be made strictly according to objective financial advice. What's more difficult to figure out is the best way to place your investments. Automatic savings plans and passive investing (not chasing after performance) are generally understood to be beneficial for most investors over the long term.

In terms of spending money, it's clear that people prefer to spend money when they spend it on something they enjoy. For this reason, I recommend you get excited about the things you *don't* feel like saving up for. This is very different advice from telling you not to be emotional when it comes to your money. I don't think that's a realistic expectation. I'd like to think most people would be capable of manipulating themselves into new spending patterns if it meant a greater chance at long-term financial success. This idea stemmed from a client who told me a story about why he didn't purchase his dream car: His son was a few years away from college and tuition was a looming expense. Rather than buying the $50,000 car he'd planned on, he decided to buy a $20,000 car and sock the extra money into a college savings plan instead. This, he figured, would ultimately encourage his son's success and resulting desire to buy his father the dream car he always wanted. Realistic? Maybe, maybe not, but it allowed him to think positively about the future and make a better financial decision as a result.

For More Information

The blogs listed for this chapter all share one particular quality: Rather than focusing strictly on investment advice, they pay close attention to the personal finance issues we all grapple with in our lives. Bloggers who can do this consistently tend to attract new users who continuously join their conversations.

I've found that J.D. over at www.getrichslowly.org/blog does a great job of communicating about real-world financial issues. J.D. proudly publicizes the fact that his blog is to be used as a discussion forum and source of information rather than a place to host marketing gimmicks and push products.

Another great read is http://iwillteachyoutoberich.com. Ramit, a very talented and active blogger, shares his thoughts on personal finance and entrepreneurship. While the blog is geared toward a younger crowd, anybody who visits will find a few topics of interest. One of the first features that brought me to this blog was the interview series, which always has unique guests.

Jeremy, over at Generation X Finance (www.genxfinance.com), runs an excellent blog as well. His aim is to bring sound financial advice to a new generation of investors, who will be facing different, and perhaps more ominous, questions about their future and financial security. The thoughts and ideas presented on his blog are often closely aligned with my own.

Web Hot Spots

www.getrichslowly.org/blog
http://iwillteachyoutoberich.com
www.genxfinance.com

CHAPTER

9

Why Should I Open an IRA?

If you qualify, contributing money to an individual retirement account (IRA) is one of the best ways to save for retirement. For some people, including myself, it is one of the first investment vehicles they'll ever learn about. Others may stumble upon the IRA for a number of reasons: They are looking for a place to stash extra money after maxing out their 401(k), their employer doesn't offer an adequate retirement plan, or upon retirement or separation from service they need a place to roll over their retirement funds.

There are two types of IRAs: traditional and Roth. While the Roth rules have been gaining in popularity recently, I'm going to focus most of my discussion on the traditional IRA. I believe this will help you better understand the tax benefits of IRA investing before dealing with any Roth confusion.

So, let's sort out what the benefits are to opening an IRA. Then we'll figure out where to open one and how to pick investments.

What Are the Benefits to IRA Investing?

If eligible, contributions made to a traditional IRA are deductible from your gross income. That's a huge benefit, which deserves a clear illustration. If an investor earns $40,000 and contributes $4,000 to an IRA, their income tax will be based on $36,000 instead. If that investor is in the 28 percent marginal tax bracket, the individual has just reduced income taxes by roughly $1,120. However, there is another great reason to contribute money to an IRA: Capital gains, interest, and dividends that are realized from investments aren't subject to taxes until withdrawn. If the $4,000 investment from the example increases to $12,000, no tax would be due on that $8,000 gain. If you invested outside the IRA, you would owe a capital gains tax on the $8,000 in profits. Depending on your tax bracket, that could cost you several thousand dollars. (Please note that a lower maximum tax rate on capital gains and dividends would make the return on the investment more favorable, thereby reducing the difference in performance.)

Are There Any Catches?

At this point you may be wondering why the IRS, considering its demand for tax dollars, would allow this investment vehicle to exist. The short answer is that private savings by individual investors will help the government deal with future issues surrounding retirement funding. As we are quickly learning, and you will read in Chapter 26, Social Security is having problems of its own. It can no longer be relied upon as a primary income source during retirement.

The government isn't giving you the IRA benefits for free. Investors must adhere to the strict rules regarding contributions and distributions if they wish to avoid penalties associated with early withdrawals. One of the more important rules is that withdrawals taken prior to age 59½ are subject to a 10 percent penalty. Plus, the money becomes taxable income in the year one takes the distribution. Keep in mind that distributions always become taxable income in the year they are taken, whether at age 30, 60, or 80. (As mentioned, the age at which the 10 percent early withdrawal penalty disappears is 59½.)

There are a few exceptions to the 10 percent penalty, such as using the money to buy your first home or using the money toward certain qualified higher education expenses, but the rules are few and far between. There are also some so-called hardship withdrawals that may allow you to avoid the penalty as well. These exceptions are equally few and far between, and you probably wouldn't want to be in a situation in which you qualify for a hardship withdrawal. All the rules and regulations associated with IRAs boil down the fact that the IRS offers these tax incentives with the intention of helping you create a nest egg. If you aren't ready to commit any dollars to retirement, it's probably best to save outside of the IRA. It's also important to remember that there may be changes in tax rates and tax treatment of earnings that lead to different results. Investors should consider their personal investment horizon and income tax bracket, both current and anticipated, when making investment decisions.

My brother is one such investor who prefers not to utilize the IRA vehicle. He feels that the lack of liquidity prior to reaching age 59½ makes it a less attractive investment vehicle—especially to people in their 20s and 30s. He would rather pay tax than lose access to funds until the distant future. What he's really saying, if you read between the lines, is "Why should I save for my retirement when I'm 30 years old?" This is an important question, fairly common, and understanding the answer could be one of the keys to your future financial comfort. Yes, most people hope to be wealthy one day, and I hope my readers achieve that goal. However, the times and places in which you will acquire money in your lifetime are extremely difficult to anticipate. Investing when you're young is a fabulous thing to do, whether $1,000 or $100,000.

Take the following example, which illustrates the time value of money. Let's say John Doe accumulates $10,000 before age 30. Then he decides to get married, have two children, and take out a mortgage. John might find that it becomes increasingly difficult for him to save money as he takes on more obligations, regardless of higher earnings. If he had even $10,000 saved before age 30, the impact of compounded growth would be substantial. At a 9 percent annual return, starting at age 30, gross of any fees or expenses, that $10,000 would become $132,677 by age 65.* If he invested that $10,000 at age 50 instead, it would be worth only $23,674 at age 65. Like I said, time is a tremendously important component of investing. And, if you think of it this way, the IRS is actually doing you a favor by putting such rigorous restrictions on withdrawals.

How Do I Find an IRA?

Assuming you're convinced at this point that opening an IRA and saving through it will help you reach your financial goals, let's figure out the best way to do this. As an adviser, I can tell you that it's not

---

*This hypothetical illustration does not represent any specific investment.

all that difficult. Pick up the phone and call your financial adviser (if you have one) and tell him or her that you want to open an IRA. For a new account, mutual funds will likely be your best option. You won't have to worry about choosing investments, because mutual funds are professionally managed. If you pick a good family of funds, you will have plenty of options for later on when your portfolio is larger and requires a wider variety of investment choices. When you first start out, one fund will generally be sufficient. Your time frame and risk tolerance will naturally have an impact on your investment selections as well.

Brokerage accounts may be another interesting option for opening a new IRA, although I tend to think brokerage IRAs are better for IRA rollovers than they are for new accounts. I will go into more detail about this in the rollover chapter (Chapter 10), but the short version of it is this: Brokerage accounts give you great flexibility in that you can choose from a world of investments; however, they can get sticky with commissions, fees, and transaction costs if you're not careful. Although brokerage accounts may actually reduce your costs in some situations (generally when you have more money), they could increase your costs when your account is fairly new and doesn't have too much money in it. You must investigate your situation carefully before making this kind of decision.

You can also open an IRA directly with your bank. Banks tend to be my least favorite place to initiate investments, as they often have limited products and work on commission. That being said, the investment minimums at banks are often quite low for people just starting out. Again, mutual funds will probably be your best option. There are even certain mutual fund companies that you can call directly to open up the IRA without paying a sales load. This will often be an excellent and inexpensive choice. However, paying a small sales load may be worth it to you if you have a favorite mutual fund company, or a trusted adviser whom you prefer dealing with.

What Kind of Investments Should I Buy?

Once you've decided on where to open your IRA, you must choose how to allocate your money. Obviously, this is going to depend on your tolerance for risk more than any other factor. Once you determine that, usually through a questionnaire of some sort, you must consider that IRAs have features that will make certain investment options more desirable than others. For example, IRAs are generally long-term investments. Money that might be required for daily needs or emergencies should never be kept in an IRA. This is what checking and savings accounts are for. Generally, more volatile assets such as stocks and corporate bonds are appropriate investments. Also remember that bond interest that gets paid into your IRA is not subject to taxes. That should be understood as "Don't invest in tax-free bonds in your IRA." You may as well buy corporate bonds that are paying higher rates if you can withstand a bit more volatility. I can't tell you the frustration I feel when I notice an investor utilizing tax-exempt or tax-friendly bonds in an IRA.

Anything Else to Remember?

There are a few other things to keep in mind that will be helpful for your traditional IRA investment. The government puts limits on the amount of money you're allowed to stash away. In 2007, $4,000 is the maximum. If you're over age 50, you're allowed an extra $1,000 catch-up contribution. There are also income phaseouts that could disqualify you from contributing to an IRA. If you are single and have more than $50,000 in adjusted gross income (AGI), or married and have $75,000 in AGI, you probably will not qualify for a traditional IRA. The logic in place is that your right to a tax incentive should be eliminated once you are earning above certain thresholds.

Furthermore, you must start taking distributions from your IRA once you reach age 70½. The government's intention is to prevent you from keeping the IRA growing on a tax-free basis forever. The government allows the tax-deductible contributions in the first place to provide you with a savings incentive for retirement, not to provide tax-free money to your children or grandchildren, whom the government would like to pay tax. There is a table that explains what your required minimum distribution (RMD) is starting at age 70½. It is technically possible to get around this rule as well, but that's a more complicated discussion. What you need to remember is that you can start taking penalty-free withdrawals after age 59½ and you must start taking withdrawals by age 70½.

The Roth IRA

The preceding discussion has dealt primarily with traditional IRAs. However, the Roth IRA exists as well, and puts a spin on things. Considering how popular it has become, I recommend doing your homework prior to making a decision about which IRA to utilize. The Roth IRA still allows your money to grow tax-free; however, rather than taking a tax deduction at the time you make contributions, you fund the IRA with after-tax dollars and don't have to pay income tax when you eventually take distributions.

It's debatable whether the Roth IRA, with the tax benefits coming later on in life, is better than a traditional IRA, which offers the tax benefit at the time the contribution is made. The answer depends entirely on your individual situation, and even then it's often hard to make the assessment. The benefits that should come to mind immediately with the Roth IRA are that you don't have a required minimum distribution (RMD) at age 70½ and the income phaseouts are slightly higher than with the traditional IRA. You'll definitely want to refer to the Internet for a more complete discussion of Roth IRAs. If you have a 401(k), you may already be seeing the new Roth 401(k) plans debuting in your office. These will operate similarly to the regular Roth IRA: Your salary deferral will be after-tax, rather than pretax (smaller paycheck), but you won't have to pay income taxes when you eventually take distributions.

For More Information

The Internet loves discussing IRAs. Because tax laws that affect eligibility and contribution limits tend to change every few years, lots of debate goes on about how to handle IRA investing. Plus, the advent of Roth products generated substantial buzz on its own. For general information on IRA investing, visit www.fool.com. The Motley Fool is a financial community that became very popular in the late 1990s covering individual stocks. I enjoy the site because of its laid-back style and amusing columns. Not only are the authors talented and knowledgeable, but the content library is excellent as well.

In terms of blogs, plenty cover IRA and other related topics in the personal finance arena. Two blogs of particular excellence are www.mymoneyblog.com and http://www.theskilledinvestor.com/wp. The latter site, run by Larry Russell, is an incredible resource. His blog has loads of original content and links up with popular stories from all around the Web.

If you want more detail about the Roth IRA (which there seems to be demand for lately) take a visit to www.rothira.com. Don't be intimidated by the huge library of content on the home page. You'll

find lots of interesting material here. You can also reference www
.investopedia.com, a site that works fabulously for this chapter and
also works well for the other topics on investing. Not only is Investopedia an encyclopedia of terms, but it also has a very practical aspect
to it. When you search for a term, the site gives you technical information along with an "Investopedia says" comment that is usually
quite useful. Searches also bring up related articles for each search
term, which, to my amazement, always seem to anticipate my very
next question.

Good luck with your IRA! May it grow and prosper!

Web Hot Spots

www.fool.com

www.mymoneyblog.com

www.theskilledinvestor.com/wp

www.rothira.com

www.investopedia.com

CHAPTER

10

What's a 401(k) Rollover?

IS THAT SOMETHING I CAN TEACH MY DOG?

P at yourself on the back if you're leaving a job and have questions about your 401(k). If you do, it means that you took the time to establish a 401(k) account at work. By doing so, a portion of your pay was directed into a tax-deferred vehicle that allowed you to accumulate funds, presumably for retirement. You didn't *have* to save through the 401(k), but you did because you either understood its benefits or heard it was a good idea.

A 401(k) rollover refers to moving a 401(k) plan from a former or current employer into either an individual retirement account (IRA) or another qualified plan. You are most likely not required to consolidate your retirement accounts into an IRA, but many people choose to do so for a variety of reasons. If you contribute to several 401(k) plans in your lifetime, you may find yourself doing a rollover more than once. Let me explain further some reasons why one might decide to do this.

Why Should I Roll Over My 401(k)?

Your first inclination may be to cash out your existing 401(k) funds. Think twice before taking this option. You're most likely going to get penalized if you take a withdrawal from your funds prior to age 59½. Assuming you were contributing to a traditional 401(k) plan—and not a Roth 401(k)—you'd be responsible for paying the tax on the money you put into your plan plus a 10 percent early withdrawal penalty. There are a few exceptions to the penalty, but they are few and far between and usually the result of a severe hardship need. Part of the reason IRS rules are strict regarding early withdrawals is that they are strongly discouraged because most people will need the money in their 401(k) to be a supplement to other income sources during retirement.

Something else to consider is the convenience and ease of management that comes along with consolidating your accounts. If you receive statements from multiple fund companies, you might be less inclined to review each one promptly; you may simply add them to your "financial stuff" file, which you may not review often enough. For some people, consolidating accounts will improve their ability to manage investment activity. It may lead to potentially beneficial financial practices such as rebalancing your portfolio and updating your asset allocation more frequently. Because your risk tolerance may change at various stages of your life, it's important to know which risks are associated with the investments in your 401(k).

The largest potential advantage, in my opinion, of rolling your 401(k) into an IRA is reducing your expenses. Not all 401(k) and IRA plans have high internal expenses, but many do. Further, while the majority of 401(k) rollovers are into mutual funds, you may have the option of rolling your plan into a self-directed brokerage IRA. Assuming you can work out a reasonable fee schedule with your adviser, using low-cost products such as index funds and exchange-traded funds may be the way to go. The impact of high brokerage fees is often overlooked by investors, and eventually can lead to disappointment or regret about how a portfolio was handled.

This is ironic in that fees and expenses are among the few aspects of your investment accounts that you can actually control. You can't make the Dow Jones Industrial Average move up on a Tuesday just because you'd like to have a big day in the market. The seemingly random movement of investments is affected by a multitude of factors, many of which are macroeconomic in nature and beyond the realm of your control. Thus, your focus should be on your personal risk tolerance, how your funds are invested, and any costs that might reduce your investment return.

Let me give a hypothetical example of how high fees can put a strain on your investment performance. Imagine two investors, both looking for growth in their portfolios without taking on too much risk. One employee decides to leave his 401(k) with a former employer upon switching jobs, invested in subaccounts through a variable annuity platform. The other employee rolls his 401(k) over into a fee-based brokerage IRA. The annuity owner would continue to pay mortality and expense (M&E) risk charges along with internal expenses on the mutual funds. According to the National Association for Variable Annuities, the average total expenses for variable annuities are about 2.32 percent.* Yes, that's about $2,320 per year on a $100,000 account. The other investor, working with a fee-based brokerage account, has the 401(k) in an index fund with an expense ratio of 0.18 percent per year. That's about $180 per year. Needless to say, the annuity owner in this example would be sacrificing a substantial chunk of his total return to various fees, expenses, and sales charges. The index fund investor, assuming he was paying only transaction costs and a nominal fee to his adviser, would stand to keep a lot more of his investment returns. In light of this, vocalizing your questions about fees, expenses, and sales charges should not feel uncomfortable at all: We are talking about your retirement funds, aren't we?

One other item worth thinking about when considering a rollover to an IRA is the potential for your former employer to become distressed, merge with another company, or bring about any other situation that you couldn't really anticipate. This returns to the rollover benefits of convenience, control, and ease of management. By consolidating your accounts to an independent third party, you will have an easier time monitoring them. If your former employer changes its 401(k) plan or merges with a new one, your account could be transferred to a platform that you don't like as much.

Are There Any Reasons *Not* to Do the Rollover?

The way I see it, you may as well have the best possible platform when it comes to storing your nest egg. If your former employer had an excellent, low-cost 401(k) plan with which you had only positive

---

*National Association for Variable Annuities, "The Real Cost of Variable Annuities," June 2004.

experiences, the rollover might not be necessary. This scenario would most likely occur in a large corporate setting that has the money and management expertise to offer a plan with top-notch administration, investment options, and customer service. In practice, not everyone works for a Fortune 500 company, and many of those who do are confused and intimidated by their retirement plan. That being said, there are a couple of instances that could either complicate the rollover process or make it less desirable.

If you work for a publicly traded company, you may own stock in your 401(k) plan. If you're not buying stock directly with your salary deferrals, the company may be matching your 401(k) contributions in the form of stock. This type of arrangement can be mutually beneficial for the employer and the employee. If the company grows and is profitable, the stock price could appreciate. More important, if employees are compensated in company stock, they have an incentive to work hard and further immerse themselves in the culture of the company. If you have a plan that operates like this, it could complicate the rollover process. You'd need to move the 401(k) to a custodian that can accept stock in addition to mutual funds. This would generally be a brokerage account as opposed to a mutual fund company. You could probably sell the stock to quickly resolve the issue, but that might not be your desire.

The rollover question could also be complicated by an outstanding loan at the time you wish to move your funds. Each plan has different rules regarding loan provisions, which you'll want to investigate prior to borrowing the money from your account. As a general rule, if you don't pay back a loan within 60 days of rolling over your plan, the loan may be treated like a distribution, resulting in both taxes and a 10 percent IRS penalty. Some plans fully restrict the movement of 401(k) funds until loans are paid in full and the account is in current status.

Investing money in a company 401(k) plan is an excellent way to save for long-term goals. In fact, many advisers recommend that their clients save the maximum amount possible through 401(k) and other retirement plans prior to opening up other investment accounts. This is advice given primarily from a tax standpoint. Why should you subject yourself to capital gains tax, ordinary income tax, or both on money you won't need until the future? Leave it in your retirement plan, let it grow, and plan for your future!

For More Information

In terms of helpful web sites, I would recommend you visit www. 401khelpcenter.com. This incredible resource is run by Rick Meigs, a pioneer in the retirement plans industry who brings valuable information to the fingertips of plan sponsors and participants. His web site is unbiased, and I often find myself nodding in agreement with the research found within.

If you're looking for the hard facts about 401(k) plans, you can get a great introduction at www.about.com. While I try to expose smaller sites that deserve publicity, about.com is a tremendous resource that stays true to its name. At the end of each article, related topics and articles are offered for further research.

For a more vibrant perspective, the blogosphere covers 401(k) issues with a hands-on approach. You'll get to read individual experiences and get varying perspectives on how to handle questions regarding investment options, expenses, and a host of other topics. I'd recommend, once again, visiting http://allfinancialmatters.com. JLP has a multitude of posts on 401(k) plans and related retirement issues. One reason I enjoy this blog is that it features stories from magazines and newspapers and links to them on the blog. This is actually a fundamental aspect of blogging, but some are more consistent at it than others.

Another great blog can be found at www.1stmillionat33.com. The author, Frugal, shares his vision of wealth and has unique content on retirement and investing. To find specific information on the site, you can either read through the archives or use the search box on the upper right to save yourself some time.

Web Hot Spots

www.401khelpcenter.com

www.about.com

http://allfinancialmatters.com

www.1stmillionat33.com

11

What's the Difference between a 401(k) Plan and a 403(b) Plan?

I field a lot of questions regarding the various rules that govern 401(k) and 403(b) plans. Not only is it a confusing topic for the average investor, but the issue has been gaining in importance recently as these plans become a central focus of retirement planning. The reason their titles seem similar (which often confuses people) is that both reference the section of the tax code that defines how they are organized. It may be easier to refer to them as "for-profit" and "not-for-profit" retirement plans since that is the primary distinction.* Here we'll discuss some of the similarities and differences between the two plans, along with reasons people use them.

If you work at a for-profit company, you may already have a 401(k) plan available to you at work. If you don't have a 401(k) or any other retirement plan available, you may wish to bring this up with your employer. Most financial advisers would agree that utilizing company retirement plans has become more important recently in light of future uncertainty regarding government benefits. The 403(b) is available only to tax-exempt organizations, the most common of which are schools, hospitals, and religious groups. Section 501(c)(3) of the Internal Revenue Code contains ample detail about which organizations qualify as tax-exempt.

---

*A nonprofit can technically offer a 401(k) plan, although it's not very common.

What Are the Tax Benefits?

Participants set aside money on a pretax basis through the company payroll. Let me explain what that means: If $100,000 was your taxable income for 2006 and you deferred $10,000 through payroll into either a 401(k) or a 403(b), your taxable income would be reduced to $90,000. This is the primary benefit of contributing on a pretax basis.

The deferral amount, $10,000 in our example, is directed into your retirement plan. In the case of the 403(b), you may have a selection of plan providers to choose from. I will discuss this selection process further on in this chapter, as there are things you should know about where to direct your money. If you get paid monthly and you have 12 pay cycles per year, $833 would be taken out of each cycle and deposited into your account.

The money invested in your 401(k) or 403(b) plan grows tax-deferred until you take a distribution, presumably at retirement. It is important to note that the age at which you can take a penalty-free distribution is 59½. If you take a distribution before this age, similar to an IRA, you likely will be subject to a 10 percent early withdrawal penalty. Assuming you had contributed a total of $50,000 to your plan and it grows to $100,000 through the years, you would not have to pay capital gains tax on that appreciation. In this scenario, you saved money by contributing to the plan on a pretax basis while you were working, *and* your assets grew without the burden of paying capital gains tax. Those are some nice benefits, don't you think?

What Are the Other Primary Features?

As I mentioned, the choice of which company administers your retirement plan will be an important factor throughout the time you are contributing. Both 401(k) and 403(b) plans come in a wide variety, generally offered through mutual fund and insurance companies. Participants in a 401(k) typically don't have a selection of plans. Once an appropriate 401(k) plan has been decided upon by the firm's executives, the only choice for the employee is whether to participate. This keeps matters simple and provides a certain level of uniformity within the plan.

One example of why this uniformity is important is for ease of administration. Consider the necessity of such a uniform system for plan features such as matching contributions. Many 401(k) plans offer employees the benefit of employer matches. Not only does employer matching provide an incentive for employees to save more, but the employer qualifies for a tax deduction based on on how much it matches.

Considering the importance of this 401(k) feature, I'd like to give a brief example of how it works. Assume a company matches half of your contribution up to 3 percent of your salary in a given year. If you earn $100,000 and deposit $10,000 into your 401(k), your employer would answer with an additional $1,500 (half of 3 percent or $3,000). In essence, this is free money. Most financial advisers will encourage you to research the rules regarding matching contributions and make them an early priority in your retirement planning efforts.

Administrators of 401(k) plans are often subject to strict legal requirements in terms of monitoring both the contribution levels and the investment activity of the participants in their plans. Many of these requirements are the result of the Employee Retirement Income Security Act (ERISA) of 1974, which was designed to improve disclosure and protect employee interests. In some cases, a 403(b) plan may sidestep ERISA requirements. An example of this would be a plan in which the salary deferrals are solely at the discretion of the employee, as is the method in which they are invested, and no matching contribution is being made by the employer. In this case the employer has little involvement in the plan arrangement, short of announcing that the plan is available.

The 403(b) works quite differently from the 401(k) in that often a variety of plan options is available to the employees. Typical vendors may include an annuity platform through an insurance company, as well as a variety of mutual fund companies, some with sales loads and some without. If an option with no sales load is open to you, this is most often the way to go. As we discuss in the annuity chapter (Chapter 21), the insurance platforms often aren't worth their costs because one of their primary benefits, tax deferral, is already inherent in the 403(b) vehicle. The employer or organization will generally provide a list of its registered 403(b) vendors for you to choose from. In the event that you don't like the options available to you, getting a new vendor registered to your organization may be an option as well. Contact your plan administrator for more information on how that process works.

Anything Else I Should Know?

Some plan providers offer other convenient tools as well. Questionnaires to determine a proper asset allocation are becoming increasingly popular, as is the ability to rebalance a portfolio throughout the year to maintain your target allocations. As we'll learn in the chapter about asset allocation and rebalancing (Chapter 22), these features tend to be the central focus of many investors, even ahead of security selection. Rebalancing is often praised for helping to smooth out volatility. It also prevents too much money from accumulating in one asset class. Further, research shows that portfolio rebalancing may improve performance over long periods of time.*

Even more significant, in my opinion, is having access to proper investor education. If you participate in a company retirement plan, there is probably somebody you are allowed to speak with who will answer questions you may have about your plan. This is very important, as a small mistake could result in penalties or negative tax consequences. I'm in the business, and I still run into questions regularly that require me to reference the tax code or a lawyer.

The 90-24 Transfer

The 90-24 transfer rule (named after IRS revenue ruling 90-24) allows 403(b) investors to move their funds to other plan providers while still in service at the same employer. A common reason people may decide to do this is if they are unhappy with some aspect of their current plan. It may be the investment options (or lack thereof), service from the current provider, or some other reason. In order to utilize the 90-24 transfer, both your current plan provider and the new vendor must be authorized to process this sort of request. If you're in a plan that doesn't allow it, you may be out of luck. If it does allow it and you have a specific company you wish to work with in the future, call the other company to see if it is able to process your transfer. You may just get the news you're looking for.

There are a few quick things to keep in mind about this process. You should always check with your current provider about what the sales charges or other fees may be if you move your account elsewhere. Sometimes these charges can be steep enough that it's not

---

*Bernstein Global Wealth Management, "The Science and Psychology of Rebalancing," www.bernstein.com.

even worthwhile doing the transfer. Also, you cannot take possession of your funds during the transfer, even for a brief period of time. The 90-24 transfer is trustee-to-trustee, meaning the individual investor cannot intercept the funds, even if only for a couple of days or weeks.

If you wish to redirect future salary deferrals, remember to update your payroll department as to your changes. If you forget and a few dollars are deposited with your old provider, you may have to go through the transfer process all over again.

What Are the Contribution Limits?

The recent passage of the Pension Protection Act made permanent certain contribution limits defined in the Economic Growth and Tax Relief Reconciliation Act (EGTRRA) of 2001. These limits are $15,000 for 401(k) and 403(b) plans if you're under 50 years old, and an additional $5,000 (up to $20,000) if you're over 50. These limits will be indexed for inflation beginning in 2007. You gain penalty-free withdrawal access to your retirement funds when you turn age 59½. There are a few exceptions in which you can access your money prior to age 59½ without getting penalized, such as if you arrange for 72(t) withdrawals* or if you either become disabled, die (in this case your beneficiary will likely get your money), or have a qualifying hardship withdrawal. The hardship withdrawals include a few scenarios such as needing to pay for a medical emergency that you otherwise couldn't afford. The withdrawal rules are few and far between because the goal is that you let the nest egg sit and grow. However, some plans do have loan provisions under which you can borrow against your account; however, check with your benefits department to determine if this feature is available to you.

For More Information

There are numerous resources on the Web that are available to help you navigate retirement plans. As we mentioned in Chapter 10, www.401khelpcenter.com is a fabulous resource for questions you may have regarding your 401(k). The site is user-friendly and doesn't make any endorsements that could jeopardize the site's credibility.

---

*Section 72(t)(2)(A)(iv) of the federal tax code provides an exception for payments that are part of a series of substantially equal periodic payments made for the life of the account holder and his or her designated beneficiaries.

For questions regarding 403(b) plans, www.403bwise.com is the authoritative site. It has excellent discussion forums trolled by experts who will answer your questions about 403(b) plans. This site is run by Dan Otter, a former teacher who has done an excellent job of encouraging investor education and spreading the word about low-cost investments. Otter co-authored a book, *Teach and Retire Rich* (bWise Guys, LLC, 2005), with Scott Dauenhauer, a fellow financial planner and blogger. Dauenhauer writes two excellent blogs: http://themeridian.blogspot.com and http://teachersadvocate.blogspot.com. These are both bookmarked on my ever-growing list of favorites.

If you're looking for broad news about the retirement planning environment, such as news on legislation and current trends among the plan sponsors, visit www.plansponsor.com. The information and resources on this site are extremely comprehensive. While the site is geared more toward financial professionals, the information can benefit anybody who drops in to click around.

Web Hot Spots

www.401khelpcenter.com

www.403bwise.com

http://themeridian.blogspot.com

http://teachersadvocate.blogspot.com

www.plansponsor.com

12

How Do I Pay for College? (Part I)

BORROWING MONEY FOR MY FUTURE

When I first suggested a chapter about college savings to a friend of mine, he responded that it might not be a topic with broad enough appeal. It took me about five minutes to realize how untrue that is. In fact, I can't think of an age group that isn't attached to at least some aspect of the college process.

Children, from a very young age, are in a competitive environment that demands all sorts of college preparation. Junior and senior years of high school are obviously some tough times with the rigorous admissions process and plethora of confusing financial questions. After college, many people end up paying off loans until around age 40, having started shortly after graduation. Around the time many of us will finish paying back student loans, we must consider the funding issues that surround our own children.

I've divided this chapter into three age groups that I think appropriately categorize the broad networks of information that apply. The first and largest section is geared toward young people aged 14 to 18. It covers preparing for college and dealing with scholarship and financial aid questions. The next section, for ages 18 to 22, covers financial opportunities available while in college, along with organizational ideas that could help after graduating. The following section, aimed at the 22-to-40 crowd, deals with the issues of consolidating and paying off student loans.

Essentially, this chapter is about getting the extra money, after personal savings, that you may need to pay for an education. Chapter 13 will address investment products and ideas that exist to help you *save* for higher education. As with retirement, the government, which tends to support education, encourages using certain investment vehicles and provides incentives to those who do so.

I'm in High School. What Should I Do? (Ages 14–18)

This is the best of times and the worst of times for many young people. During high school, financial obligations are presumably minimal for students; their primary responsibilities are managing schoolwork and getting involved in extracurricular activities. The goal is to remain competitive in an increasingly cutthroat college admissions process. Some families do include working and earning money as important responsibilities during high school. Whereas I appreciate the message sent by parents who promote financial responsibility in high school, allowing students the time and freedom to explore academic opportunities with minimal strings attached, if possible, may prove more valuable over the long run than having them stress about earning money.

Paying for education is an equation with fairly predictable solutions. Following these solutions will often lead to myriad opportunities while one is still quite young. To be financially savvy, students should open dialogues about scholarships, grants, and financial aid shortly after entering high school. They should then choose a college that is the best fit for them considering a range of factors from educational opportunities to location and price. Upon entering college, students should work hard, further develop their personalities, and explore career options. The world is a bit less scary with good preparation.

The three primary sources of financial aid are scholarships, grants, and student loans. There may be other forms of aid that are available to you as well, but these three, because of their widespread popularity, will be our primary focus.

Scholarships

There are all sorts of ways to reduce full tuition at both public and private universities. Some scholarships are offered directly by the college if you fall within certain criteria regarding grades, standardized test scores, class rank, legacy, or awards. Schools offer these both as incentives for students to strive for higher standards and to increase the prestige of the institution. If a college can brag that, on average, its undergraduate students graduated in the top 25 percent of their high school classes, this will enhance the reputation of the college and its standing in the global landscape.

Scholarships are also offered by a variety of smaller organizations. Sometimes a fraternity or sorority will set up a scholarship fund that rewards applicants who are expected to enter the organization and become active members. These scholarships are often funded by wealthy alumni who want to support an institution that positively influenced them during their younger years. A good way to learn about scholarship opportunities is to contact the college financial aid office of your choice directly. You can learn from them what scholarship opportunities are offered by the school and how they can be accessed.

Several resources exist on the Web to help with this type of search. To locate the contact information for most college financial aid offices, search on www.finaid.org. This site is a comprehensive source of student financial aid information. Two other sites that help simplify the scholarship search are www.fastweb.com and www.studentscholarshipsearch.com. Both of these sites allow you to customize a search for various scholarships and other forms of financial aid. There may also be regional scholarships, which can be learned about from a high school guidance counselor, local religious group, or private individual.

Grants

Grants, like scholarships, are ideal in that they don't need to be paid back. If you could find a way to pay for college through scholarships and grants alone, you'd probably be in great financial shape upon graduating. College applicants are often awarded grants simply by filling out the Free Application for Federal Student Aid (FAFSA) during their senior year of high school. The FAFSA can be found at www.fafsa.ed.gov. When you receive your FAFSA awards summary, it will outline grants you received from various organizations. While grants are awarded to many people, including those with excellent academic qualifications, they are based predominately on financial need. Those with hardships are likely to see a larger percentage of grant dollars from most academic institutions.

The Pell Grant is the most popular need-based federal grant. The maximum Pell award for 2006–2007 is $4,050, but this amount can change with political administrations and new legislation. If you wish to obtain a grant from your state, it may also be awarded with your FAFSA package. However, I'd recommend contacting your choice schools for more information on whether your state has specific application criteria of its own.

Grants, similar to scholarships, may be offered by a corporation or private foundation with a specific purpose. Perhaps company X offers 10 annual grants of $2,000 for students who excel in mathematics. You may wish to contact the company for an application to apply for its grant. Remember, it takes a little effort to make these things happen.

The FAFSA application makes life a bit more convenient but won't cover all your bases. I've spoken with several organizations that offer grants that aren't particularly well publicized, and often there are only 10 or so applicants for three or four grants. This means free money for every few people who apply! The way to find out about financial award programs that aren't well publicized is to contact an organization you wish to get involved with and ask if anything is available. Two thumbs up for grants if you can get them.

Student Loans

It's time to get realistic. While we all hope that scholarship and grant dollars cover a substantial portion of our tuition, student loans are the only way many of us will be able to pay for college. The popular federal loan programs, which you may have heard of, are Stafford and Perkins.

Stafford loans can be awarded as subsidized or unsubsidized. This refers to whether or not the government will cover the interest charges while the borrower remains a student. Subsidized loans are generally preferred because the interest doesn't begin accruing until a few months after one graduates. Stafford loans are need-based, but reasonably accessible in terms of availability to the middle class as well. Stafford loans generally have competitive interest rates, which makes them more appealing than other types of loans.

Unsubsidized Stafford loans also have competitive interest rates but are not predominately based on need. A family with adequate college funding that prefers to finance a portion of college tuition can do so with these loans. However, borrowers should be aware that they are responsible for interest accruing on the unsubsidized loans while in school. This puts a bit more pressure on the borrowers.

Perkins loans have a similar structure and are quite useful as well. The U.S. Department of Education gives a specific amount of money earmarked for Perkins loans to qualifying schools. The school then determines which students have the greatest need. The school combines federal funds with some of its own funds when disbursing these loans to students. Like Stafford loan rates, the interest rates on Perkins loans are substantially lower than on private or alternative loans. Filling out the FAFSA, like much of the other financial aid, is the way to learn if any Perkins loans are available to you.

I Filed My FAFSA. Now What?

Once the government sends you back your awards summary based on the information you submitted in your FAFSA, you'll have an idea of how the government recommends you structure your college financing. Obviously this is to be used just as a guide, since the FAFSA form can't anticipate each person's unique financial position.

One will often notice in the summary that a Parent Loan for Undergraduate Students (PLUS loan) is recommended. These are essentially student loans for parents. They have fairly high interest rates, and the repayment period begins shortly after borrowing the money. PLUS loans are designed to cover what's necessary to pay for college after scholarships, grants, student loans, and the expected family contribution (EFC) are tallied.

The EFC is the amount the government determines parents should contribute to their child's education. At this point you may be thinking, "How does the government make this sort of determination?" You'll understand the answer quite clearly when you sit down to fill out the FAFSA. On that form you will reveal your family's financial situation in detail. This helps the government understand your finances and determine what sort of financial aid package you deserve. As a word of caution, I wouldn't recommend fibbing on the FAFSA for any reason. Besides breaking the law, you put your financial aid package at risk if the government can prove you haven't provided the most accurate information available to you.

I'm in College. Do I Still Need to Focus on Money? (Ages 18–22)

When a student is in college, it is hoped that most financial demands will already be in order. Getting good grades and exploring internship and work opportunities should become the primary focus. On a financial note, sometimes a student can participate in work-study programs that can be applied toward tuition.

Work-study jobs have a reputation for being on the easy side as they help the college fill positions with considerable flexibility. Programs I've heard of include working at the library, admissions office, or a specific department for a set number of hours each week. Federal work-study programs are fairly common and generally pay a rate that is higher than minimum wage. In my own experience at New York University, work-study paid $10 to $12 per hour.

I'd like to close this section by pointing out situations students should be aware of with regard to managing their financing decisions while in school. Most of these points boil down to keeping an eye on scholarship, grant, and loan disbursements either online or through the student financial aid office. You want to make sure all money is paid on time and to the right place. I've seen lots of people have their classes dropped on the very first day of a semester because full tuition wasn't paid by the deadline. This often isn't even the fault of the student, but falls on his or her shoulders when a payment doesn't reach the right place at the right time. The result could be ending up in all 8 A.M. classes. Speaking from experience, this is not something a first-year college student wants to deal with. Also, certain scholarship programs require maintaining a certain grade point average to receive future funds. Don't take this lightly, as each thousand dollars you lose could impact your future. Learn what your scholarship guidelines are, and do your best to keep free money.

I Graduated. How Poor Am I? (Ages 22–40)

New college graduates must once again visit their financial situations. A few major decisions with regard to paying back student loans (if they have them) must be made. It is common that a six-month grace period will be granted to give borrowers a chance to figure out their next move, whether graduate school, a job, or moving to Tahiti. At that time one must either begin to pay back the loans, defer payment to a later date, or pursue some form of loan consolidation. Let's quickly review the three options.

Paying Back Loans

If you are happy with the terms of your loans and have the ability to begin paying them back, you may as well start. If you happen to be attending graduate school, the repayment question probably won't apply. The subsidy on most loans will continue until you either finish your education or reach a specific age. Also, I've noticed that parents will often (when possible) make the first few payments on behalf of children while they are establishing themselves in the workforce.

Federal loans often have competitive interest rates and should be paid back according to the repayment schedule. It should not be a given that you try to pay down your loans as fast as possible. Some people choose to do so because they wish to get rid of debts before focusing on savings. While ridding yourself of debt may seem like the right thing to do, it may not be. For example, if you can earn 5 percent risk-free in a Treasury bill and your student loans are costing you only 4 percent per year, you'd be better off applying extra capital to the Treasury bill rather than paying down your student loans. Granted, personal preferences do play a role in this decision as well. If you have a decent rate and the payment isn't overly burdensome, crunch the numbers and see which avenue is best.

Deferring Payment

For various reasons, including a good Macy's sale or a once-in-a-lifetime vacation, some people will be unable to begin repaying their loans within six months of graduating from college. Lenders expect this and actually don't kick up too much of a fuss about payment deferrals. This is because they continue to charge you interest in the meanwhile. I find it ironic but not uncommon that demonstrating financial hardship will end up costing you more money in the long run. However, this is the nature of the lending industry. As you become more capable of making large, on-time payments, banks will be more willing to lend you money and listen to your needs. Typical deferment periods are six months to one year, and the interest is generally tacked onto the principal amount of the loan.

Whereas I wouldn't recommend taking a deferment unless necessary, it's an important option to consider if you are trying to relocate for a job or make another financial decision that could benefit you in the long run. You always want to weigh your options carefully and choose the one that ultimately serves you best.

Consolidation

Loan consolidation is a very popular business. Various banks compete over student loans because of the interest earned by them during repayment. Consolidation programs simplify loan repayment by combining several types of federal loans (such as Stafford and Perkins), which may have different terms and repayment schedules, into one new loan. The interest rate after consolidation may be lower than the individual rates on one or more of the loans. In addition, consolidations often result in lower monthly payments and increased flexibility of the repayment period. For those who need it, a consolidation should make the loans easier to manage. A good objective source for consolidation questions is http://studentaid.ed.gov. You may be able to get information from banks as well, but be cautious about a lurking profit motive. Banks compete over consolidations because of how many students ultimately decide to refinance their loans.

Once you are consolidated, you could very well be paying off the loan until around age 40. It is hoped that your schooling has led you to green pastures and the payments don't affect you too much at later ages. Fortunately, most student loan payments can be automatically debited from your checking account, putting the process out of mind. And remember, the interest on your student loans is a good tax deduction!

For More Information

There are a bunch of good Web stops you can make, besides those already mentioned, to learn more about college payment and preparation. Check out http://blog.wellsfargo.com/StudentLoanDown. This blog is intended to be an ongoing conversation in which high school and college students can correspond with moderators about financial issues. It's a very friendly blog and a good source of free information.

The Student Loan Network is a leading online resource for topics such as student loans and financial aid. The Network sites have a lot of information, so click around slowly and carefully. I'd advise you take a look at the student loan blog, which can be found at www.staffordloan.com/student-loan-blog. It updates frequently and even has a daily podcast. The Network's financial aid blog can be found at www.financialaidnews.com, and the loan consolidation blog is at

www.studentloanconsolidator.com/student-loan-consolidation-blog.
Yes, that's a long one, but it's worth the typing.

For general information on college funding, you can always rely
on comprehensive sites such as www.about.com and http://money
.cnn.com as well.

Web Hot Spots

www.finaid.org

www.fastweb.com

www.studentscholarshipsearch.com

www.fafsa.ed.gov

http://studentaid.ed.gov

http://blog.wellsfargo.com/StudentLoanDown

www.staffordloan.com/student-loan-blog

www.financialaidnews.com

http://www.studentloanconsolidator.com/student-loan-
consolidation-blog

www.about.com

http://money.cnn.com

CHAPTER

13

How Do I Pay for College? (Part II)

SAVING IN ADVANCE

Numerous studies have been done to assess how effectively parents save for their children's college costs. The findings are fairly predictable: While many families make an effort to earmark a portion of their personal savings for educational expenses, not nearly enough money is being saved. Further, those who are putting aside money often aren't doing so in the most advantageous ways.

The good news is that savings patterns have improved over time. The bad news is that the price of an education tends to inflate at a shocking rate. So, what are we to do about all this? We learned in the preceding chapter how a family can make up for shortfalls in savings through financial aid. Now let's talk about how to make the most of our available savings vehicles so that our children can enter the world with as little debt as possible.

Why Is Paying for College Such a Hurdle?

It would be nice if a brilliant answer to this question existed that could resolve the issue for everybody. Unfortunately, it isn't quite so simple. Education, especially for private colleges, is extremely expensive. Education also happens to be an institution of utmost importance to most people, one that they fully expect to pay for. A 2005 survey by AllianceBernstein Investments found that 94 percent of parents feel that "helping with college expenses is [the] best investment they can make in [their] children's future."* The survey also found that 41 percent intend on paying their children's college costs in full.

What does this really tell us? Parents want their kids to go to college, and they want to help pay for it. The problem is that tuition costs have historically increased at a rate much higher than inflation.

When I attended New York University, my costs were roughly $38,000 per year—including tuition, housing, and books. I had an arrangement with my parents that they would pay for the first three years of college and I would pay for the final year. Whereas I jumped at this arrangement at the time, I now cringe each month when a small chunk of money gets deducted from my checking account to pay back this loan. It has given me a real understanding of how enormous these costs are and how hard my parents must have worked to make these payments for me and my brothers. I expect that 20 years from now when my kids are entering college, attendance at a school such as New York University could cost in the ballpark of $100,000 per year.

I've also learned from my clients that saving money for their children's college educations tends to overlap with the time when planning for their own retirement becomes a priority. In my ideal world of financial planning, one would try to sock money away into retirement accounts prior to having children (so these funds would be compounding from an early age), and could then divide savings between college and retirement starting when the first child is born.

 Tip: A common financial planning error made by parents is earmarking too much money for college and not enough for retirement. Your children have their whole working lives ahead of them to pay back school loans. When funds run short, saving enough money to retire should be the primary responsibility, followed by saving for college. Obviously, the earlier you start, the better off you will be.

Let us explore ways to save.

---

*"Failing Grades? American Families and Their College Saving Efforts," AllianceBernstein College Savings Crunch Survey, August 2006.

What's the Best Way to Save for College?

Burying cash in a treasure box in your backyard is probably not a good idea, but any other method you choose for accumulating funds for college, even throwing your change into a piggy bank, is a good one. That being said, some methods of saving are certainly more beneficial than others. My four favorite college savings vehicles are 529 plans, Coverdell (education) IRAs, savings bonds, and Uniform Gifts to Minors Act (UGMA) accounts. All four of these are quite different from the others, so I will explain them briefly.

Section 529 Plans

Many financial advisers argue that Section 529 plans are the best college savings vehicles. Earnings within the account are exempt from federal taxes when used for qualified higher education expenses. They are similar to an IRA or 401(k) in that you don't have to worry about capital gains taxes within the account, assuming the money is properly distributed. Many states also allow for an income tax deduction based on the size of your contribution.

Section 529 plans are convenient in that there are no income limits that restrict who can utilize this type of plan. A parent who earns $500,000 per year can still make regular contributions to the plan. The account owner retains control of the assets within the account and, if necessary, can change the beneficiary to somebody else within their family. Note that many of the rules are state-specific. Check your state's web site for a list of authorized 529 plan vendors.

Coverdell IRAs

Coverdell IRAs are also tax-exempt when used for qualified education expenses. The two downsides to these accounts are the low $2,000 annual contribution limit and the income eligibility phaseouts at $110,000 for single filers and $220,000 for joint filers. The other benefits, including ability to switch beneficiaries and having the account owner retain control over the investment options, are the same as in the 529 plan.

Series EE Savings Bonds

Series EE savings bonds are popular because they are exempt from state and local income taxes and, if used for college expenses, from federal tax as well. While notoriously boring, savings bonds are guaranteed by the full faith and credit of the federal government and are an extremely safe investment.

While I would probably recommend a 529 plan over savings bonds in most cases, very conservative investors might still prefer this style of investing. Series EE savers might get caught up in a phaseout if their income is above a certain level. These income limits vary from year to year, so it's best to consult a financial or tax adviser for the exact numbers.

UGMA/UTMA Accounts

Uniform Gifts to Minors Act (UGMA) accounts and Uniform Transfers to Minors Act (UTMA) accounts are surprisingly popular in the college savings arena, considering their relative inferiority to other savings methods. First, these accounts are taxable. Granted, the tax rate of a minor is likely much lower than that of his or her parent, but it's still higher than the exempt status one might get from any of the other three alternatives discussed. UGMA funds are also treated as assets of the child, unlike the other three savings choices. This can be a major disadvantage in the financial aid process, as discussed in further detail in the following section. Keeping these points in mind, parents and grandparents often set up these accounts to gift money. Unlike 529 plans and Coverdell IRAs, UGMA and UTMA proceeds do not have to be used toward higher education. In exchange for this flexibility, you lose some tax benefits.

Will Saving Money Affect My Child's Ability to Get Financial Aid?

Didn't think about this, did you? This section could save you lots of stress if you pay close attention. The way current financial aid formulas are set up, it actually makes more sense to save in the parent's name than in the child's. This is because a child's ability to receive financial aid, including scholarships, loans, and grants, will be affected by the amount of assets owned by the child.

Some people think that just because their children's tax brackets are lower than the parents', they should stash away money in their children's names. This can be a mistake for two reasons. The first is that a law that is in place when your child is 10 years old may change or be done away with altogether by the time that child reaches college age. The second reason is that saving some money in your child's lower tax bracket could cost your child the ability to get grants or other free money from the government. If this happens, you will be worse off for saving this way. Although obviously difficult to anticipate, this outcome can be avoided by smart planning.

To reiterate, 529 plans remain my preferred way for a relative to save money toward college. Although the beneficiary of the account will receive the money for higher education, the asset is treated as the property of the account owner, not the beneficiary. This differs from the UGMA/UTMA accounts in which the asset belongs to the student and can adversely affect a financial aid package. Similar to a 529 plan, Coverdell IRAs and Series EE savings bonds are relatively safe from a financial aid point of view because the assets are treated as the property of the account owner rather than of the beneficiary.

For More Information

Many of the links mentioned in the prior chapter are applicable to this section as well. Besides www.finaid.org, which is among my favorite broad reference sites for college finance issues, www.savingforcollege.com is fabulous as well. The latter site is geared more toward the material in this chapter, specifically the 529 college savings plan. There is a blog on the site, run by Joseph Hurley (a 529 plan guru), who shares thoughts and tips about college savings with readers (www.savingforcollege.com/joes_blog).

I've also bookmarked a site called Hoverings, which is a blog catering to the parents of children in college. It can be found at www.collegeparents.org/blog.

Web Hot Spots

www.finaid.org

www.savingforcollege.com

www.savingforcollege.com/joes_blog

www.collegeparents.org/blog

PART III

LIVING IN A FINANCIAL WORLD

CHAPTER

14

Am I Ready to Pick
My Own Stocks?

There comes a point in many investors' lives when they decide to dabble in the stock market. I consider this to be a turning point in the life of an investor, a coming of age in which one graduates from a passive strategy and demands more control over one's investments. Some people return to letting others manage their stocks shortly after trying their hand in the market because of a bad experience. Others have success or just find the process interesting and maintain permanent involvement with the stock market.

Besides the potential for profitability, researching your own stocks has side benefits as well. First, your understanding of individual corporations and the economy in general will likely improve. Also, your journey into stocks may inspire a curiosity about other areas of the investment arena such as bonds and real estate. I remember back in high school

 Tip: On the topic of research, it should be noted that Google launched a finance portal early in 2006 that is a must-see for new investors (http://finance.google.com). While loyalists may still prefer the Yahoo! portal (http://finance.yahoo.com), Google Finance has truly unique features such as interactive charting and a search tool specifically designed to navigate the blogosphere.

when I first took an interest in the stock market. I dedicated a chunk of my spare time to examining financial statements, listening to quarterly earnings reports, and researching executives to find out who's who.

I can recall when the market dabbling phase happened in my own family many years ago. My father installed a satellite dish on the roof of his dental office to give him improved access to stock quotes. Each time his stocks went up the computer would make a sound like a cash register. Each time they moved down you'd hear something of a train wreck. Ah yes, those were the days of dabbling.

How Should You Go about Picking Stocks?

There are practically as many theories about how to pick stocks as there are stocks to invest in, so the first thing you need to do is determine an investment strategy that is right for you. Will you be the sort of investor who buys a stock for life? I respect this strategy greatly but have noticed that few people have the patience or lasting desire to follow it. At the opposite end of the spectrum are day traders, who pick up stocks in the morning with the hope of gaining a few percentage points before selling them that afternoon.

I'd like to focus on the value-oriented investment approach for a moment, since this seems to be hailed by some of the most famous money managers, including the master himself, Warren Buffett. Value investing entails finding companies with deflated stock prices that may be undervalued by the market. There are numerous ratios that value investors use to view their stocks against others in the same sector of the market or some other benchmark comparison. One example is the price-earnings (P/E) ratio, which values a company's current share price against its earnings. A low P/E ratio may indicate that a stock is cheap relative to its peers. Of course, there may be some other factors (such as a pending lawsuit) that can help justify the low P/E ratio.

Because of certain complexities in the stock picking process, some investors shy away from self-picking stocks and simply follow an established approach to investing. One such example is the Dogs of the Dow. There are variations to this strategy, but let me to explain the basic concept: An investor picks the 10 stocks out of the 30 in the Dow Jones Industrial Average with the highest dividend payouts and lowest prices. Dividends, for the record, are company profits that are paid out to shareholders. At the end of each calendar year, the investor redesigns the portfolio using the new lowest-priced, highest-dividend stocks in the Dow. Utilizing the Dogs of the Dow strategy would have given you an average annual return of 13.46 percent over the 10-year period ended December 31, 2005.* Please note that no strategy can ensure success, and past performance does not guarantee future results.

Before we continue, I should make two things clear about the workings of the stock market:

1. The stock market is exactly that: a market. When an over-all lack of confidence pervades the market and feelings of uncertainty about the future exist, stocks can go down. You may even find a stock going down on a day in which the company announced good news. This sort of anomaly should not make you angry or even surprise you. It's a part of the emotional roller coaster that comes along with following stocks.
2. While many theories exist for how to obtain unusually high returns in the stock market, there is no proven method that will always outperform the major market indexes. You may find a theory that works for 10 years in a row and then turns on its head the year you decide to try it out. You might complain that it's just your bad luck, but many people will share these experiences with you.

One way to narrow down your list of stocks is by using a screener. Perhaps you read in a magazine that you should buy small-capitalization stocks with high return on equity percentages. You might have no clue what this means, but that doesn't mean you can't still follow the advice. Yahoo! Finance (http://finance.yahoo.com) and MoneyCentral (http://moneycentral.msn.com) both offer stock screening services in the investment research areas of their web sites. You can plug in data such as company size, ratios, cash balances, earnings growth, and the like. Within seconds, a list of stocks that fit your criteria will appear on the screen. You can then choose your stocks from the updated list.

Another great way to choose stocks is based on common sense. This strategy is rarely discussed in the financial community, and I think it's a good one. In 2004 I went shopping at a gourmet market on Long Island. While examining the expensive and well-packaged

*Dogs of the Dow (www.dogsofthedow.com): Annual return based on 10 dogs as of December 31, 2005.

goods, I thought about how impressive this shopping experience was relative to others I'd had. I also noticed the store carried a large supply of health and organic foods, capitalizing on the trend to eat healthy that has blossomed in recent years. This kind of thought process can lead you to a company with real profit potential.

The key to making money in this situation is to have an understanding of the time lag that exists between when a good idea is created and when it's recognized in the stock price. It turns out the market I was shopping in was indeed a publicly traded company. Needless to say, the price was lower back then and the company has grown and matured since. Once everybody else figures out the good investment opportunity, you've probably reached the time to get out of it and pocket your profit.

My girlfriend provides another interesting strategy for purchasing stocks. At the end of each calendar year, she reviews her credit card statements and buys stock in those companies in which she spent the most money. At first I laughed at her method, but later realized its brilliance. As a resident of New York City, she is exposed to many new and exciting trends when they are first introduced— often well before they gain national popularity. Further, by purchasing her stocks based only on where she shops, she isn't trying to time the buying of a stock on a day when the price is seemingly low. This works out well since many investors who try to time their purchases according to the market price end up falling into the emotional pattern of buying a stock when its price is high and selling it the second it dips down.

Her strategy has led her into some very attractive companies and subsequently attractive profits as well. One area to watch out for when utilizing this strategy is overcrowding a certain sector, in her case retail. This can be dangerous during economic cycles when certain industries tend to be more resilient than others to fluctuations in consumer spending.

Finally, a great way to research stocks is by reading the advice and experiences of other investors. This can help you avoid some of the otherwise inevitable problems that new investors tend to have. Some of these include:

- Holding on to a winning stock for too long (being greedy).
- Not knowing when to sell a losing stock ("maybe it'll come back" syndrome).
- Getting emotional over swings in the price of stock.

For More Information

There are so many great resources on the Web for investors that it's difficult to narrow down the list. Investment sites tend to have different feels to them based on the writers. When you find a few you're comfortable with, you'll often return again and again.

You may wish to start your research with a visit to www.trading-markets.com. This site is geared primarily toward traders. Its excellence is derived from the knowledge and experience of its contributors, many of whom are seasoned financial services professionals. They also run www.themoneyblogs.com, which is a blog community covering financial topics ranging from stock picking to entrepreneurship. All of this information is free and extremely useful. You can find my blog, www.russellbailyn.com/weblog, in there along with many others.

While navigating the blogosphere, http://seekingalpha.com should be on your list of sites to visit. Seeking Alpha is different from other sites in that the focus is on opinions in addition to news. Visitors come to read the thoughts of financial professionals and bloggers. In fact, some of the bloggers whom I reference throughout the book may also be contributors to the Seeking Alpha network. For those who may not follow financial jargon, *alpha* in this context is a reference to how well a portfolio is performing given a certain level of risk. Some of Seeking Alpha's notable features include:

- The ability to search for articles by typing in the ticker symbol or name of a company you wish to learn more about. This user-friendly feature makes the filtering process much easier.
- You can link to blog articles on specific areas of the market such as biotechnology, media, gold, the Internet, and Japan.
- The site has a comprehensive listing of earnings conference call transcripts. For investors who do their homework, this becomes a great resource for figuring out what's going on behind the scenes each quarter.

Whereas Seeking Alpha is more of a collective resource in terms of reading opinions, I'd like to point out some individual investing blogs that I visit as well.

- Ticker Sense (http://tickersense.typepad.com) is run by the money management firm Birinyi Associates. The blog combines stock discussion with market analysis and current trends in an easy-to-understand fashion. Ticker Sense also has a subscription newsletter that provides stock picks.

- Controlled Greed (http://controlledgreed.com) focuses on value-oriented investment strategies. Value stocks, as we mentioned, have prices that appear cheap relative to a few different analysis techniques. The site's name is a reference to Warren Buffett, who said that controlled greed is an important quality for investment success.
- Wallstrip (www.wallstrip.com) is an emerging video blog where "stock culture meets pop culture." The site does an excellent job of bringing fun back into the stock market. Howard Lindzon, the executive producer, is an entrepreneur who understands how to communicate effectively with busy people: keep it short, simple, and sweet.
- Trader Mike (http://tradermike.net) is a cool blog for swing traders and short-term stock pickers. The blog owner, Michael Seneadza, a technical trader who trades for his own account, offers watchlists, market recaps, and other helpful trading resources.

Dabbling in the stock market can be both fun and profitable if you are resourceful and do your homework. Read about the experiences of others and pick an investment strategy you are comfortable with. Remember to go back and review your strategy and risk tolerance every so often as well. A safe tactic is to make a budget dedicated to your dabbling and keep it separate from retirement accounts and other saving vehicles that are essential for your future goals.

Web Hot Spots

http://finance.google.com
http://finance.yahoo.com
http://moneycentral.msn.com
www.tradingmarkets.com
www.themoneyblogs.com
www.russellbailyn.com/weblog
http://seekingalpha.com
http://tickersense.typepad.com
http://controlledgreed.com
http://tradermike.net

15

What Are Alternative Investments?

W hat do you think of when you hear the word *investment*? Stocks, bonds, and real estate probably come to mind. I wouldn't think that hedge funds and private equity would be a first reaction for most people, although they have become increasingly popular topics of discussion. I'd like to talk about what investments are generally classified as alternative, and what potential value they add to a portfolio. There must be some good reason why billions of dollars are flowing into these asset classes, and perhaps you could find a way to benefit from this knowledge as well.

Alternative investments are unconventional in that most people don't have access to them. They're also not the sort of investments you'd see a commercial for during the Super Bowl. The publicity for alternative investments is more or less contained within the same community that utilizes them. This community consists primarily of deep-pocketed investors, such as public and private pension funds, financial institutions, and college endowment funds. Wealthy individuals can often access them as well.

There are a few explanations for why only this wealthy demographic can participate in these investment classes. However, most of them boil down to the same reason: risk. Regulators don't want to see Mr. Small Investor run short of money because a private equity transaction requires him to earmark $500,000 that can't be accessed for several years. Even worse, he runs the risk of losing the full $500,000, which could represent the majority of his net worth.

It's more than likely this type of investor couldn't handle the volatility or lack of liquidity involved with this investment class, even if he were willing to do so. Institutions, however, can often withstand great volatility and long periods of illiquidity. In fact, most pension and endowment funds *have* to plan 30 years or further into the future.

One reason ordinary investors might take notice of the alternative investment arena is that individuals such as those reading this book may soon find themselves gaining access to this unfamiliar class of investments. My feeling is that as the financial markets continue to evolve, new products will be introduced with ways of including smaller investors in hedge funds and private equity deals. We've already seen this pattern emerge in countries such as France and Australia. Also, through more traditional asset classes such as mutual funds and exchange-traded funds (ETFs), you may be able to fulfill a similar alternative investment objective.

So what are these alternative investments? The ones I'm most concerned with are real estate investment trusts (REITs), private equity, hedge funds, and commodities. There are other investments that could be included within the definition for alternatives, but these strike me as popular and often widely misunderstood. Let's tackle one at a time.

Real Estate Investment Trusts

Real estate investment trusts are securities that invest directly in real estate through a portfolio of properties or mortgage loans.* Unlike some of the other alternative investments, REITs are available to both ordinary investors and the high-net-worth markets. Because their popularity is still somewhat recent, I've included them in this chapter. Some REITs are publicly traded like stocks, while others are privately held. Investors in private REITs usually have similar objectives to those in public REITs, but face a few important differences. Private REITs don't have the liquidity or transparency associated with publicly

---

*Investing in real estate and REITs involves special risk, such as limited liquidity, changes in tax law, tenant turnover or defaults, competition, casualty losses, and use of leverage. Real estate values may fluctuate based on economic and other factors. An investment in real estate or REITs may not be suitable for all investors and there are no assurances that the investment objectives of any real estate program will be attained.

traded securities. However, shareholders will notice an overall lower amount of price volatility as a result of that. Naturally, public markets are spooked by emotion and perception, and the share prices will react to these factors. Any stock market investor can tell you this much. However, some volatility can be a blessing in disguise. If you find seemingly inexpensive REIT shares that are under the radar, you might obtain a steady income stream along with appreciation in the price of your shares.

Investing in REITs is a great way to become involved in real estate without the headache of actually buying and selling property. REITs also provide commercial exposure, which is otherwise uncommon for the average investor to deal in directly. Borrowing money for commercial transactions can be complicated, as can tenant issues regarding leasing out space. It's easier for most people to speculate on residential property, because nearly all of us are familiar with it. Nonetheless, exposure to commercial property is good for diversifying your real estate holdings, especially at a time when certain commercial markets seem to be gaining in value quicker than residential markets. REITs can also invest in shopping centers, golf courses, or even vacant land.

As a REIT shareholder, income is usually a primary objective. Considering the fact that REITs are required to pay out 90 percent of their net income to shareholders, one can feel relatively confident about receiving those payments. Some view them as a risk-reducing alternative to other income-producing investments such as bonds and dividend-paying stocks. REITs also provide an interesting avenue for diversification, one that has certainly made its way into more portfolios since 2000.

Private Equity

I get asked about private equity almost as frequently as I do hedge funds. I can understand the confusion, because private equity is a broad term that includes a variety of types of transactions. It's also not publicized in the same way as a mutual fund or insurance company might promote its products.*

---

*Private equity investors must undergo a suitability review that would qualify them as Accredited Investors.

The primary function of private equity transactions is to take a financial interest in a company and work with the management team to improve some aspect of the current business model. There are several reasons private equity firms might do this, but most boil down to increasing value for the shareholders. In practice, this process isn't easy and doesn't always work out as planned. The private equity firm might have a very different idea from the existing company executives about what represents a good or bad decision for its owners (the shareholders).

Venture capital (VC) is a common form of private equity investment. While it can materialize in a bunch of different ways, venture capital generally refers to capital infusion to start or expand businesses with excellent potential for growth. Sometimes the businesses are already profitable and the extra capital will be used to speed up the growth rate. Other times, a business may be struggling and VC funds will allow it to improve operations in the short run. Venture capital firms perform a crucial function in the expansion of the economy in that they allow smart thinkers to partner up and turn their contained ideas (they hope) into Fortune 500 companies. Successful venture capital experiments have resulted in breakthroughs for the health care, electronic, and information technology sectors, to name a few.

Venture capital deals typically mature in one of three ways: a sale, a merger, or an initial public offering (IPO). Under ideal circumstances, the sale or merger would occur after the business has grown according to plan and both the business owners and venture capitalists will profit appropriately from the deal. Sometimes the VC firm will have relationships with potential buyers in advance. Remember, some of these businesses may be quite small and finding a buyer isn't easy. Typically a VC fund might invest in 20 or 30 companies at a time, expecting only a handful of them to show returns.

Sometimes it will make sense to hold an IPO once the funded business has been properly nurtured. The business owners and VC firm stand to profit when they eventually sell off portions of their interest in the company. You may remember the open-arms treatment with which new technology offerings were received in the late 1990s leading up through 2000. Every idea, even those that didn't yet earn money, seemed to be magical. When reality set in, many of these ideas were found to be mediocre at best. Nowadays, most VC funds take on a higher level of due diligence before handing out money to start-ups without a solid financial plan.

Another form of private equity that has been turning heads for many years is the leveraged buyout (LBO). Whereas some forms of private equity aim to grow small companies into larger ones, or struggling companies into profitable ones, LBO transactions look to obtain controlling stakes in already established and often publicly traded businesses. In a typical LBO transaction, the private equity firm will locate a company that it believes to be undervalued by the market. After taking a small equity interest, the private equity firm will attempt to borrow the remaining funds needed to make the purchase, often using the assets of the company it is buying as collateral for the loans. The private equity firm will then bring in management experts to improve operations and bring back value for shareholders. LBO transactions can be friendly in the sense that they attempt to cure emerging disparities between management and shareholders, or they can be strictly motivated by profit, a pure but often controversial form of capitalism. Sometimes these moves follow a maturing business that is missing opportunities or a family firm that has grown substantially and would be better off if the founders were bought out and economic opportunities were pursued.

You may be familiar with LBOs because of the less-than-perfect reputation they developed in the late 1980s when aggressive and profit-minded private equity firms were hostilely disrupting company operations. One of the most famous private equity deals occurred in 1989 when Kohlberg Kravis Roberts, a major private equity firm, took over RJR Nabisco for $25 billion. Watch Michael Douglas in *Wall Street* if you want a dramatic commentary about corporate raiders from the 1980s.

Recapitalization is another goal of some private equity transactions. There is a variety of reasons why a business might need to alter its capital structure. It could happen to avoid bankruptcy—typically by selling off assets. This adds cash to the balance sheet, which can be used to improve business operations. It could also take place to fend off a takeover attempt. This is sort of a more interesting need for recapitalization. It could happen through the issuance of debt and a decrease in the number of a company's outstanding shares. Taking on new debt isn't always what shareholders want, but if used wisely, it can ultimately improve a company's operations.

Hedge Funds

If you ever thought that investing wasn't sexy, then you haven't thought of hedge funds. These are pools of money funded by institutions and wealthy investors, which can be applied to a wide variety of investment options. For example, while traditional mutual funds can only be long a security (buying it with hopes of appreciation), a hedge fund can be long or short (borrowing a security and selling it with hopes of buying it back at a lower price). This allows the fund to make money on the downside as well. Hedge funds can also buy options, use leverage, and program trade. These are all methods of taking on and spreading out increased levels of risk. However, they do provide the possibility of unusually high returns.*

Part of what drives the recent hedge fund rage is the lack of regulation hedge funds are subject to. Once a hedge fund has a pool of capital, it has virtually free rein as to how to invest those funds. This attracts wealthy investors who won't be satisfied with the average historical returns provided by more traditional investment classes. Like private equity, there are restrictions on who can participate in hedge funds. These barriers to entry bother some ordinary investors who may otherwise be willing to take on more risk. The one clear advantage hedge funds have over some other investments is the relaxed regulatory environment. I don't think this will last forever, but it will continue to improve the ability of hedge fund managers to perform while it does.

To be perfectly honest, I don't see hedge funds as necessarily better investments than individual stocks, bonds, or mutual funds. Hedge fund investors simply take on more risk, which often leads to extraordinary returns, especially when they take on leverage. It doesn't always work out so well, though. An incident in mid-2006 with Amaranth Advisors, a Connecticut-based hedge fund, demonstrated just how risky these vehicles can be. A natural gas trader missed on a heavily leveraged bet and cost the fund several billion dollars.

The way hedge fund managers get paid is an interesting and somewhat controversial topic as well. Unlike traditional mutual funds, which usually charge only annual expenses, hedge fund managers get performance fees as well. Let me put into perspective just how much money we're talking about. If a hedge fund manages $1 billion and charges a 2 percent management fee, the fund is

*You should carefully investigate any hedge fund since there could be limitations and risks, such as limits on payouts of returns, illiquidity, and non-diversification of the portfolio. Of course, all hedge fund investing involves risk, including loss of principal and fluctuation of investment return.

collecting $20 million before performance bonuses. If the fund returns 20 percent in a given year, or $200 million, the manager may get another $40 million (20 percent) in addition to management fees. This may shed some light on why so many young people are trying to strike while the iron is hot in the hedge fund industry.

Commodities

Did you know that markets exist to hedge against the price volatility of commodities such as oil, cocoa, wheat, and oranges? It's actually a great way to diversify an investment portfolio and place wagers on future events. However, because of the complex and speculative nature of this investment style, it most often falls into the alternative investment category alongside private equity and hedge funds.*

Commodity investments are often made through *managed futures*. This name reflects the fact that professional money managers trade the contracts on exchanges for investors. Each contract requires the delivery of a specific commodity, currency, stock index, or other item at a specified date in the future. Unlike options, where the buyer has the choice of whether to exercise the contract, futures imply that the buyer will take ownership of the underlying commodity at a specified date in the future. Both parties take on high levels of risk, as futures markets are a zero-sum game—one side bets correctly and the other side bets incorrectly. Plus, commodity prices can be very volatile. Take, for example, the oil bull market that has been taking place since 2003. As friction increases throughout the Middle East, people are more willing to lock in today's prices for oil. This will give them protection in the event the price of a barrel of oil moves higher. The other side of that equation is a possible oversupply of oil, which could relax prices considerably in a short period of time.

Besides investor speculation, commodities offer a very important hedging function. Those most concerned about the volatility of oil prices mentioned earlier are industries that rely on oil—airlines being a prime example. If they anticipate prices are moving higher, they might buy managed futures contracts as a measure of protection.

---

*Investing in commodities involves special risks, including increased susceptibility to adverse economic conditions and geopolitical situations that may adversely impact the sector. There can be no assurance that, at all times, a liquid market will exist for offsetting a futures contract that you have previously bought or sold.

Farmers often use futures contracts as well to protect themselves from bad weather, poor harvests, and the lower prices that might follow.*

Why the Sudden Craze for Alternative Investments?

So, why are ordinary investors all of a sudden taking an interest in these alternative investment classes? There are a few explanations, but my feeling is that *diversification* is the dominant reason.

As I've mentioned throughout this book, having a diverse portfolio of securities is one of the most valuable recommendations I can make to an investor. If you put all your eggs in one basket and your basket breaks, all of your eggs will crack. Thinking this way about your investments is a key element to obtaining long-term wealth. And it doesn't apply just to financial investments. If I derive 90 percent of my income from one fabulously rich client and the two of us have a falling-out, I'm now facing a big problem resulting from my lack of diversification. If I can balance my practice like I do my portfolio, I'm better protected against risk. But, how do we achieve *really* good diversification?

Traditional methods of diversification would have us buying various asset classes with neutral and negative correlations. For example, owning a portfolio of stocks, bonds, and REITs would be more beneficial from an asset allocation point of view than owning only stocks, only bonds, or only REITs. We might also diversify within asset classes, perhaps buying gold and precious metals stocks because they tend to have low correlations relative to other U.S. equity sectors. That being said, these theories are designed to smooth out volatility, not to provide total protection from a bear market when everything seems to be headed south.† Vehicles such as the hedge fund can provide substantial gains for investors, even if the markets are uniformly moving down. This is a major opportunity for portfolio managers to offer value—if they are good at what they do.

---

*Options involve risk and are not suitable for all investors. Prior to buying or selling an option, a person must receive a copy of Characteristics and Risks of Standardized Options (ODD). Copies of the ODD are available from your broker, by calling 1-888-OPTIONS, or from the Options Clearing Corporation: One North Wacker Drive, Suite 500, Chicago, IL 60606.

†Asset allocation strategies do not assure a profit or protect against a loss in declining markets. No strategy can guarantee the objective or goal will be achieved.

The need for diversification is further emphasized by the rapid transfer of information and the trend toward globalization. As the world continues to connect, investors may want to consider looking beyond simply owning U.S. equities. We are becoming more vulnerable to actions abroad, and as these vulnerabilities become more consistent and predictable, we should consider how these actions could affect our investment portfolios. Unfortunately, only wealthy and institutional investors can capitalize on the majority of investment opportunities discussed in this chapter. However, this has slowly begun to change in the past five years, and I'm hoping more opportunities for alternative investing will present themselves in the future. It certainly seems logical, considering the pace at which financial markets evolve and become more efficient.

Ordinary investors may soon gain exposure to hedge funds, as a few have been talking about going public. To my knowledge, at least at the time I'm writing this book, there aren't any publicly traded hedge funds. In terms of private equity, ordinary investors already do have a way to gain access. An exchange-traded fund (ETF) was released in 2006 that tracks publicly traded companies that invest in private equity. What a novel idea! It's not a direct play, but it does give retail investors a chance to capitalize on the huge profit potential derived from the private equity deals done by these companies. Of course you'll want to consider what else these public companies are doing, but it's a start. An ETF could be used to provide commodity exposure to a portfolio as well.* You may not get the leverage typically associated with managed futures, but you will get the diversification. Keep your eyes and ears open for news about evolving products that give individual investors access to alternative investment markets.

For More Information

This is a fun chapter for blog features. I particularly like venture capital blogs because they talk about the newest technologies and give readers a glimpse of what may be the next important innovation.

---

*ETF investing involves risk. Please see Chapter 17 for additional information.

"A VC" (http://avc.blogs.com) is a blog written by Fred Wilson, a venture capitalist from New York City. Fred is a success story from the dot-com era, and his posts are diverse and amusing. Take a peek if you're interested in tech gossip, but expect to read whatever topic Fred feels like commenting about that day. Good food for thought here.

Brad Feld has a really great blog at www.feld.com/blog. Feld is a venture capitalist from Boulder, Colorado, with a rich history in technology investing. I particularly enjoy his posts about entrepreneurship. Most of his writing has a free-flowing style that is fun and easy to grasp.

If you'd like to read the "Sardonic Memoirs of a Private Equity Professional" visit Going Private at http://equityprivate.typepad. com. This blog has an extremely wide range of content stemming from a very clever author. It strays outside the world of private equity on many occasions but in good taste. Check this one out and you'll keep coming back, too.

If you're curious about hedge funds, take a glance at http:// hedgefund.blogspot.com. This is one of the best reads for background information and commentary on hedge fund investing. It's written by industry expert Veryan Allen. The blog has an educational feel to it and poses the sort of questions a hedge fund investor might want to know about.

To learn more about the commodities markets, I would take a look at www.commoditytrader.com. Commodity Trader provides a blog format to keep ordinary investors and financial professionals in the loop about the commodity markets. The blog has a stated purpose of educating investors about the global commodity markets and showing how this type of investing can decrease your risk and be used as a hedging tool, rather than strictly for speculation.

Web Hot Spots

http://avc.blogs.com
www.feld.com/blog
http://equityprivate.typepad.com
http://hedgefund.blogspot.com
www.commoditytrader.com

CHAPTER

16

How Do I Pick Mutual Funds?

A good financial adviser will try to explain concepts in such a way that clients can really grasp the knowledge. As obvious as that may sound, many people who work with financial advisers do not learn much about how to make financial decisions; they merely pay to have those decisions made for them.

Mutual fund investing is one such financial concept that all investors should know about. If you haven't already, you'll likely encounter mutual funds at some point during your financial life through either your individual savings or a company retirement plan. According to the Investment Company Institute, which compiles statistics on various investment classes, currently over $9.5 trillion is invested through more than 10,000 mutual funds in the United States.* In fact, many retirement plans *require* their participants to use mutual funds rather than individual stocks to prevent them from taking on too much risk. Imagine if inexperienced investors decided to put the full balances of their 401(k) plans into the stock of a single company. What if the company became distressed or went bankrupt? They could say good-bye to their retirement nest eggs, possibly forever.

My own first taste of the stock market was with mutual funds, because I knew they were professionally managed and didn't require very large initial investments. That turned out to be a great decision, as I still have my mutual fund investment and contribute to it monthly.

---

*Investment Company Institute, "Trends in Mutual Fund Investing," August 31, 2006.

So, what exactly do you need to know about mutual funds? We'll start with the basics and then jump into more detail.

What Are Mutual Funds?

Mutual funds are pools of managed money. Their primary purpose is to provide easy access to diversified portfolios of securities. Upon buying shares in a fund, you are really buying smaller position in the underlying securities. Depending on what the fund's style is, you might be purchasing stocks, bonds, Treasury bills, or any other allowable securities. Some mutual funds may be smaller, with only a few million dollars under management, while others may have thousands of shareholders, and the total assets of the fund could be well into the billions. A small percentage of the fund's assets, generally 1 to 2 percent, is deducted to pay management fees and other operational expenses.

When you buy shares in a fund, you are essentially hoping for the underlying investments to do well. This is in part determined by how good a selection job the fund manager is doing. Some managers obviously perform better than others, but jumping into a fund that is having a good year does not mean you're bound to make money. In fact, while looking at trailing performance over 5- and 10-year periods tends to be a popular performance measure, it doesn't create any real guarantee as to future results of a fund.

The more important question to ask, prior to selecting a particular mutual fund or portfolio manager, is how you view *your own* tolerance for risk. This is essentially your willingness to watch your portfolio move around, both up and down, without becoming anxious or being tempted to redeem your shares. For some investors, the stock market is just too volatile; they may prefer bond funds or even money market funds, which are more conservative in nature and generally produce stable streams of income.

After you decide on the proper mix of mutual funds, you can start digging into which specific fund families you like best. This process is difficult for a lot of investors because they may find 10 or more fund families that offer a similar type of fund. Does it really make a difference which mutual fund family you choose? Obviously some will outperform others each year, but again, choosing among fund companies for performance is anything but an easy task.

What you can look for with a bit more accuracy is a certain fund culture or sense of style. Some companies tend to have more aggressive portfolio managers who take risks, while others stick to index investing. Understanding the basic investment policies of a fund family may help guide you in the right direction if you know what you're looking for.

What Are Some Different Types of Funds?

Once you've investigated your personal risk tolerance and decided to purchase mutual funds, you'll need to understand the financial jargon attached to them. It would be easier if funds had names like "fund for conservative men in their 30s" or "technology fund for greedy youngsters with money to burn," but that's not how it goes.

Mutual funds have standard terminology. In a typical retirement plan, you'll quite possibly see some of the following names:

- *Large-cap growth funds.* These funds invest in companies that seek growth. A fairly standard characteristic of these types of companies is that they reinvest earnings in the business rather than paying them out to shareholders as cash. The technology sector is a good example of a place to find growth stocks. A common understanding of these funds is that they offer you a great opportunity for profits, but come with a large amount of risk. *Large-cap* traditionally indicates that the underlying companies have market values of $5 billion or more. Growth funds can also be mid-cap, small-cap, or even micro-cap. These are smaller companies that you may or may not be familiar with.
- *Large-cap value funds.* Rather than seeking rapidly growing companies, value managers seek out stocks that they believe should be trading at higher prices. This might include a company that makes a hefty profit but was in the midst of a lawsuit. Perhaps investors got tired of tracking progress on the lawsuit and the stock price didn't resume a fair valuation after the suit was settled. Spotting these sorts of inefficiencies within stock prices is what could potentially make a good value manager.
- *Blend funds.* These funds invest in a mix of growth and value stocks. They typically use a comparative benchmark such as the S&P 500 or the Dow Jones Industrial Average as a measure of their success. If they are outperforming the benchmark by

several percentage points each year, the manager is considered to be doing a good job. If they are falling short of it, investors are losing out because they could have purchased a low-cost index fund instead, which would have produced a higher return. Blend funds are good for those who want an opportunity for growth along with the reassurance that their funds aren't being invested too aggressively.

- *International funds.* Why stick purely to companies based here in the United States? There are plenty of companies making money overseas as well. Managers understand these opportunities and have designed funds that invest in stocks located outside the United States. There are plenty of variations on international funds, such as emerging markets, which are generally considered riskier because they invest in young economies. Global funds invest internationally as well but they may include U.S. stocks. Naturally, hold on to your seat if you invest in risky international funds. Whereas they may pay off, you're playing with all sorts of risks, including currency fluctuations and potentially unstable governments.
- *Sector funds.* These are mutual funds that invest predominantly in a single area. Sector funds tend to be more volatile than a broad market fund because the stocks have a very narrow focus; however, the risk level depends entirely on the sector. Utilities might not be considered as scary as emerging technologies. Some investors jump into a sector fund when they believe that sector is about to perform extremely well. An example of this would be investing in oil since 2001 when turmoil has pervaded the Middle East. Other investors choose sector funds as a hedge against other mutual funds in their portfolios. Some familiar sector funds may include financial services, health care, utilities, gold, and individual countries.

Why Might Mutual Funds Sometimes Receive Negative Press?

What we haven't talked about yet is why some people are so opposed to investing in mutual funds. We can consolidate the opinions of most of these people with two related factoids. The first is that mutual fund ownership tends to be expensive. The second is that mutual fund managers, on average, have not shown such outstanding returns to their investors. In fact, many have returned less to investors than investors would have gotten had they bought low-cost index funds instead.

How are these two related? Well, if you're paying both mutual funds' expenses and a commission to your broker, you're probably looking for some sort of return. If your funds don't perform well, and they also get reduced by various sales charges, fees, and expenses, you're not going to be a happy camper. For this reason, many investors stick to low-cost index investments.

What Else Should I Know?

Now that you have knowledge about what mutual funds are, what you can expect from them, and how to decipher some financial terminology, which funds are right for you? As I mentioned earlier, your own tolerance for risk will likely be an important factor in choosing a fund.

Two other important factors are the purpose and time frame for your investment. For example, if you're buying a fund today that you will contribute to every year until you retire, you may want to consider funds with at least a little exposure to stocks. The reason is that you can withstand a bit more volatility than somebody who needs the money in six months to buy a home. If you are trying to make a diversified portfolio of funds, speak to your adviser about finding a good fund mix that gives you adequate exposure to the market and isn't overly expensive. Remember, those expenses reduce your investment returns and add up over the years.

 Tip: For reviews of thousands of different mutual funds, visit www. morningstar.com. Morningstar has a really neat system worked out for evaluating funds and separating them into appropriate categories.

The Internet offers a multitude of spots where you can find a fresh perspective on fund selection and investing. Try not to be too sensitive to any one opinion when entering a discussion about mutual funds, because not everyone offers as balanced a discussion as I do. Some investors may have entered the market with a technology fund in 2000, only to have found it lost 50 percent of its value within a year. This doesn't make mutual funds bad, just the experience of the individual investor.

Three of my favorite web sites for relatively unbiased information are www.yahoo.com, www.about.com, and www.investopedia .com. As mentioned, I would also recommend taking a look at www .morningstar.com. Morningstar, one of the market leaders in mutual fund analysis, also has a fascinating little discussion forum you can search for on the web site that was created for the self-proclaimed "Vanguard Diehards." These are fans of the Vanguard school of thought who offer advice and host discussions about financial topics. You can also access the forum at www.diehards.org.

In the blogosphere, at least at this point, no individual blogs have been written that strictly focus on mutual funds. However, a lot of the best personal finance blogs cover mutual funds and related topics in ample detail. I would refer you back to www .consumerismcommentary.com or www.freemoneyfinance.com for an informed opinion about a variety of mutual funds topics. Do your homework! Then, we hope, you can make some money.

Web Hot Spots

www.morningstar.com

www.yahoo.com

www.about.com

www.investopedia.com

www.diehards.org

www.consumerismcommentary.com

www.freemoneyfinance.com

CHAPTER

17

Exchange-Traded Funds: What Are They, and Should I Buy One?

An exchange-traded fund (ETF) is a basket of securities that trades on an exchange like a stock. In the event you don't know how the stock market works, shares of public companies trade at various prices based on demand. The distinguishing factor with an ETF is that, rather than representing ownership in a single company, it tracks an index such as the S&P 500 or Dow Jones Industrial Average. The price of an ETF, similar to a basket of stocks in a mutual fund, will vary based on the performance of its underlying holdings. If an ETF represents an index with 30 different companies and all of them are trading up on a given day, the offering price of the ETF will move up accordingly.*

A good starting point for better understanding this important and relatively new investment product is to view its advantages against other investments that could be utilized by a similar audience. Mutual funds are the investment product most analogous to ETFs that can be used as a benchmark for comparison. Let's analyze some of the criticism given to mutual funds and then see how exchange-traded funds stack up.

---

*Equity-based ETFs are subject to risks similar to those of stocks; fixed income ETFs are subject to risks similar to those of bonds. Investment returns will fluctuate and are subject to market volatility. Shares may be worth more or less than their original cost when sold. Foreign investments have unique risks, and greater risks than domestic investments. Past performance is no guarantee of future results.

- Mutual funds tend to be expensive.
- Mutual fund prices are figured only once daily—after the close of the market. If you put in an order for a mutual fund at 9:45 in the morning, you'll get the 4 P.M. price.
- An investor cannot buy options on or short sell mutual funds.
- Mutual funds often have steep sales charges.
- Most mutual funds are actively managed.

Keep in mind that, while mutual funds may have certain disadvantages, they are still an extremely popular and important investment vehicle. Part of the value that can be extracted from the preceding chapter on selecting mutual funds is based on both the staggering amount of assets invested in mutual funds in the United States as well as the fact that many retirement plans, such as the 401(k), require the use of mutual funds by plan participants. I'm highlighting their criticisms for the purpose of making my ETF discussion as clear as possible. That being said, let's talk about how exchange-traded funds are different from mutual funds.

Exchange-traded funds are relatively inexpensive. Because ETFs track indexes, their expenses are usually lower than those of mutual funds. There are several reasons for this. First, they avoid costs associated with hiring portfolio managers and research analysts to help pick securities. Second, transaction costs are typically lower as well. Unlike mutual funds, ETF sponsors do not sell shares directly to the public. They exchange large blocks of shares, known as creation units, for the securities of the companies that comprise their underlying index. In a sense, it is the predictability of the creation units that differs from mutual funds and causes fewer transactions. With a mutual fund, it is nearly impossible to anticipate who will buy shares and who will redeem shares from day to day. This operational difference also lends itself to certain tax advantages, such as lower rates of capital gain distributions getting transferred to investors.

Exchange-traded funds can be bought or sold throughout the day. Imagine if the market was rapidly declining because of a terrorist threat. Investors could sell their ETF shares early in the morning whereas mutual fund shares could not be liquidated until the end of the day. This advantage is referred to as *liquidity.*

Some people actually claim this as a disadvantage because it encourages a higher volume of trading in funds that are often intended to be purchased as long-term investments. I don't think of this as a specific disadvantage of ETFs, but rather a commentary on the impulsive and often emotional nature of many investors. Having a smart financial adviser and self-discipline should help overcome the desire to trade your core portfolio holdings.

You can trade options on or short sell exchange-traded funds. If you're looking for a potentially inexpensive way to hedge yourself after a recent climb in the markets, short-selling an ETF may provide that possibility. This practice is not possible with open-end mutual funds, as they are not securities that can be bought or sold on an exchange. One can also buy or sell options on an ETF the same way as with a stock. For example, buying a "put" on an ETF that tracks the S&P 500 index might provide some protection against a decline in the overall markets.* Similarly, if it were your belief that the broad market averages were going to perform well in the near future, you could buy a "call" on an ETF that corresponds to the market index that you'd like increased exposure to. To learn more about options strategies and how they may pertain to your portfolio, visit www.cboe.com.

Exchange-traded funds don't have steep sales charges.† How much of an advantage this is depends in many ways on your current compensation arrangement with your broker or adviser. Technically, an ETF is purchased like a stock. An investor pays a commission to a broker for executing the trade. The size of that commission obviously is something you work out with your broker or adviser, but it's likely to be much cheaper than an up-front commission on a mutual fund. For a $10,000 purchase, an ETF could cost you just a few bucks. A standard up-front commission for an equity mutual fund could run you in the ballpark of 5 percent, or $500.

Exchange-traded funds are not actively managed. The fact that ETFs try to duplicate an index rather than outperform it could be perceived

---

*ETFs can be constructed to represent the holdings found within an index; however, the trusts may not be able to exactly replicate the performance of the indexes because of trust expenses and other factors. Investors cannot invest directly in an index. Options involve risk and are not suitable for all investors. Carefully consider whether options are appropriate for you in light of your experience, objectives, and other financial circumstances.

†Depending on the number of trades executed, the cost of the associated commissions may outweigh the low expense ratio associated with ETFs compared to mutual funds. As such, in some instances, costs of ETFs may be greater than that of mutual funds.

as either an advantage or a disadvantage. The answer reverts back to the popular argument of whether actively managed funds are worth their higher level of expenses. Certain managers are famous for consistently outperforming their peers. If we knew which managers would beat their benchmarks each year, most people wouldn't bother reading articles about exchange-traded funds. However, statistics show that, over the long run, mutual fund managers usually don't beat the index to which they compare their returns.* I consider passive management an advantage for ETFs insofar as you're still getting broad market exposure but paying a fraction of the price of a mutual fund for it.

Why Else Might I Buy an Exchange-Traded Fund?

Another popular use for exchange-traded funds is to gain exposure to specific market sectors. One may do this because of familiarity with a certain slice of the market or simply to speculate on events that might cause one sector of the market to perform better than others. Just remember when overweighting a specific sector of the market that it could disrupt a mapped-out asset allocation. Investing in a specific market sector also has unique risks, including increased volatility.

Because ETFs have seen such a dramatic increase in fund flows over the past several years, they have started to evolve into quite the trendy product. Originally, ETFs tracked primarily the major market indexes such as the Dow Jones Industrial Average or the Wilshire 5000, and major sectors such as financials, health care, and technology. Now, besides the more traditional indexes, ETFs exist for various unique and alternative indexes. There is a clean energy ETF for people looking for a cheap way to gain exposure to the alternative energy market. There is also a currency ETF, a leisure ETF, and even one that tracks stocks that recently started trading publicly in initial public offerings (IPOs). Granted, it sometimes feels like too many ETFs have been released into the marketplace, but it's doubtful investors will complain about this, as it gives them a wider variety of investment options.

I find the popular reception of ETFs as trading tools to be an intriguing concept. When I first learned about this product, I immediately thought of it as a substitute for mutual funds, as discussed earlier.

---

*William Sharpe, "The Arithmetic of Active Management," *Financial Analysts Journal* 47, no. 1 (January/February 1991): 7–9.

With all the people in the world who criticize actively managed mutual funds and advocate the low-cost environment associated with index funds, you'd think ETFs, which are potentially cheaper than index mutual funds, would attract a heavy flow of funds away from mutual funds. Now, this has happened to some extent, but not with the sense of urgency I would have expected. Mutual fund assets in the United States currently stand at over $10 trillion, while ETFs are still hovering around $400 billion.*

I believe one explanation for this could be how they are marketed—both by the ETF companies and by financial advisers. Many ETFs are based on indexes that are speculative and attract investors with a high tolerance for risk. These are often the same people who enjoy trading stocks. It's questionable how many of these people are focusing on the costs of their long-term investment holdings. If they are, why haven't they embraced ETFs for that purpose as well?

Also, financial advisers who work on commission tend to make less money selling exchange-traded funds as long-term holdings than they do from selling load mutual funds. Considering the fact that many individual investors learn about new investment products through their advisers, this could certainly slow the passage of information. As we mentioned, those who are actively seeking newer investment products tend to be the investors who focus on short-term trading. So, basically, we lack a medium through which ordinary investors can learn about the potential cost savings associated with ETFs. This is one way the blogosphere can really come in handy. It's a source of free information that can potentially improve your decision making and make you a better investor.

For More Information

We've gotten through the gist of what an ETF is. Whether or not you should buy one, like most financial concepts, will depend in part on your own preferences as an investor. Compared to other investment products, ETFs generally don't attract all that much criticism. Individual investors, institutional investors, and financial advisers use them because they're typically inexpensive and easy to trade, and they provide broad access to the markets.

---

*Investment Company Institute (www.ici.org): Mutual fund assets were $10.84 trillion as of 12/31/2006; ETF assets were $383.3 billion as of 10/31/2006.

We mentioned Seeking Alpha in Chapter 14, and it applies here as well. In addition to articles on individual stocks, Seeking Alpha is among the web's best sources for reading information and opinions about exchange-traded funds. The section of the site dedicated exclusively to ETFs can be found at http://etf.seekingalpha.com. Part of the value added with a site like this is that each post allows readers to comment on the articles and leave a link back to the writer's own web site. This adds to the enjoyment of reading opinions because rebuttals and interesting feedback are sitting just below the article. If you like a specific comment, you can visit the web site of the person who left the comment and see what else that individual has to say.

Another excellent site is found at http://etfconnect.com. Rather than providing individual opinions like Seeking Alpha's ETF blog does, ETFConnect.com is a more technical site, providing quick access to data about exchange-traded funds. The site will give you information such as the objectives of a fund, annual returns, various holdings, trading volume, and dividend payout information. It's definitely a site to bookmark for future reference for technical information for ETFs.

There are two other quite different sites that are great resources for ETF information as well. The first is www.indexuniverse.com. This site is run by Jim Wiandt, a pioneer in the world of indexing. You can access product and market developments related to ETF investing or subscribe to either of the site's excellent publications.

In the blogosphere, Random Roger has really stepped up to the plate in 2006. He runs a stock market blog that is quite active (updating multiple times daily) and has great discussions about ETF investing. You can find his blog at http://randomroger.com.

Web Hot Spots

www.cboe.com
http://etf.seekingalpha.com
http://etfconnect.com
www.indexuniverse.com
http://randomroger.blogspot.com

18

Can I Dabble in Real Estate, Too?

Someone once asked me what the best investment one can make is. While this is a fairly subjective question, I answered *real estate*, and I think many others would as well. Countless fortunes have been derived from land ownership and real estate investing, including my favorite example: In 1626, Peter Minuit bought the island of Manhattan from the Indians for the equivalent of $24. It would be quite difficult to quantify what Manhattan is worth now, but let's just say he didn't overpay.

I would consider real estate the best possible investment regardless of statistics that show that the total return of the stock market over the past 50 years is actually more impressive than that of the real estate market. The primary reason for my assertion is that we live in real estate and often factor mortgage payments into our budgets. Also, a home cannot be instantly converted to cash the way a stock can and therefore has a greater chance of not being sold and consequently of building up equity. Besides this *advantage of illiquidity*, real estate can also be leveraged. Most real estate sales don't require the full purchase price to be paid up front. Often 25 percent, 10 percent, or less will be enough money down to take possession. We'll go into exactly why leverage is such an important advantage, and we'll also touch on mortgages briefly in this chapter and more heavily in the following chapter. Even though reading on about mortgages for a while can make you sleepy, the mortgage one chooses can have a significant long-term effect on one's financial health.

The most basic form of real estate ownership is your primary residence. Those who rent might notice that every month they send a chunk of money off to somebody else who *owns their home*. I'm not going to totally bash renting, for two reasons: First, during volatile housing markets renting can actually be a safe alternative to buying a home. Also, some people can't afford to buy and therefore shouldn't be discriminated against for renting. That being said, given the evolution of the mortgage industry, it's easier now than ever to secure a home, often without having to put in a down payment. At some point, many renters get frustrated with the process and decide to buy a home. This often happens when one gets married or has children, and the need for a home increases.

What Are the Advantages of Owning Real Estate?

Statistics show that the purchase and eventual sale of a home tends to provide many retirees with a necessary source of revenue. After the kids grow up and leave the house, downsizing often makes sense and a portion of the home proceeds can be used to supplement government programs such as Social Security (more on that later). Here are some other advantages to owning real estate.

Appreciation Potential

While appreciation is never a certain thing, real estate has been one of the more reliable places to park money during the course of history. Part of this is due to the consistently healthy pace at which the economy has grown. There are a multitude of reasons why this happens, including a large and productive labor force, a stable government, and technology advances. The beauty of real estate ownership is that you can benefit from the expanding economy simply by holding on to your property.

Your location will most likely contribute to the rate of appreciation as well. A friend of mine lives in an apartment building in New York City that recently converted the ground floor into a luxury food market. Apartments in the building instantly became more expensive as a result. Similarly, if a corporation decided to build a huge corporate park in a city that employed 4,000 people, you might notice an increase in demand for property in that neighborhood. These are the sorts of things real estate investors may speculate on.

Income Potential

Whereas many people buy homes to live in, others buy them as investments that will produce monthly income and, they hope, appreciate in value as well. I have a friend who recently bought a two-family home instead of a single-family home. His logic was that he had saved enough money to provide the down payment for the two-family home, so why not buy it and then rent out half the house? The renters would more than cover half the monthly mortgage payment, and he'd try to find reasonable tenants who wouldn't drive him too crazy. So far, his strategy has worked out exactly as planned. The real estate market has held up nicely in his area and he's two years into payments on a $700,000 home. He hopes the home will continue to appreciate and he can realize a nice profit when the property is eventually sold.

 Tip: For tips on owning property for income, check out The Landlord Blog (www.thelandlordblog.com). The site goes into detail on a variety of real estate investment strategies and gives a fresh, candid commentary on the intricacies of being a landlord.

Leverage

Leverage, the ability to borrow a large sum of money with a relatively small down payment, is perhaps the greatest advantage to owning real estate. Understanding why could improve your decision making regarding real estate forever.

Consider the following hypothetical example, which is both realistic and an accurate reflection of the recent market. It's 1997 and you're 30 years old. You have secured a job in Miami paying a stable $75,000 salary and managed to save a nice chunk of money while sharing an apartment with an old friend. You've decided to buy a condominium that costs $350,000. The monthly payment, including taxes, is about $2,400. You determine this to be a reasonable monthly payment, considering your job stability and responsible spending habits. The building requires that you put down 10 percent ($35,000) on the condo. You move in, decorate the place, and get comfortable.

Six years later you and your significant other decide to have a child. You agree that a suburban home is more appropriate than your current condo and decide to put it on the market. In 2003, you get a bite for your asking price, $600,000. The 72 payments you made since 1997 totaled $172,800, of which $45,000 was paid into the principal and $127,800 was paid to the bank as interest. While the interest is a bit painful, remember that you did get to live in a $350,000 home for a mere 10 percent down. You can think of all the bank interest as if it were rent. After paying back the bank $305,000 (your purchase price less your paid-down principal) and giving the broker a $10,000 fee, your proceeds are $285,000! *This* is the advantage of leverage. You might now go and put $100,000 down on a million-dollar home.

With a leveraged purchase, even though you secure the home with only a fractional down payment, you are still entitled to the appreciation that occurs. Granted, home prices don't always appreciate so quickly, and in some cases they may depreciate. However, history has shown that if you pick a good location and are patient, the opportunity to profit awaits.

In fact, in the late 1990s you didn't need much patience, because home prices were soaring in many parts of the United States. Some people believe that the real estate market has gotten way too hot in recent years. More details about this bubble phenomenon are discussed in the blogs referenced later in the chapter. Obviously there are a bunch of different takes on the current status of the market and whether we're headed up or down from here.

Lack of Liquidity

Logically speaking, an asset that takes a long time to sell should be less expensive as a result. This is why I will include this same attribute in my list of disadvantages as well. My reasoning for considering lack of liquidity an advantage, though, is more psychological in nature, a reaction to the impulsive nature of consumers regarding spending. If it's difficult to sell a home, it's more likely to be held for a longer amount of time. Some financial advisers refer to homes as "forced savings vehicles" for this reason. The longer the homeowner makes payments, the more equity will build up. This equity can be used to purchase a bigger home, supplement retirement savings, fund an education, or achieve any other large financial goal.

What Are the Disadvantages to Real Estate Investing?

Before you go out and start buying property, let me emphasize that real estate investing isn't all fun and games. Without careful planning, you could end up in hot water. Part of this "real estate can't lose" mentality stems from the blazing hot market we've seen since the early 1990s. In fact, with a few exceptions, real estate has been hot for decades. However, at the time I'm writing this chapter, there is plenty of talk about overly speculative purchasers and bursting bubbles in the housing market. Let's throw around some of the disadvantages of investing in real estate to see where one might get caught up in some trouble.

 Tip: A great blog to visit if you want to feel like a real estate insider is www.curbed.com. Covering multiple cities, Curbed exposes real estate politics, neighborhood news, and gossip, all through a user-friendly blog format.

What distinguishes an investment in real estate from an investment in the stock market is that you own a real, tangible item. Maybe you didn't buy a house, but you bought five acres of land; either way you're now exposed to the potential risks that are associated with owning real, tangible assets.

Maintenance

Whether *you* live in the house or someone else does, the homeowner is ultimately responsible for maintaining the property. If you've ever owned a home, you may have noticed that repairs aren't cheap: A new boiler, reshingling the roof, replacing the garage door, and most other common repairs all cost a pretty penny. In theory, some of these improvements could raise the value of the home, but it's often difficult to anticipate the amount of appreciation a repair will yield.

Some homeowners take out either lump sums or lines of credit against the equity in their homes to finance home improvements, pay for major maintenance, or refinance some other form of debt. While home equity can provide a good vehicle for consolidation or a tax-advantaged loan, always think twice before borrowing money from your home. Besides owing interest, it is possible for a home to depreciate in value between the time you borrow the equity and the time your home is sold. This could create a not-so-pleasant situation.

Tenant Liability

Many properties are purchased for the purpose of renting them out. The logic goes as follows: take out a mortgage; rent out the house for an amount covering the mortgage, taxes, and maintenance; and watch the home appreciate in value while others make the payments for you.

Now, this situation is realistic and does happen all the time. In fact, some people used this strategy back in the 1980s to buy big buildings, which they now own entirely. Besides paying tax, much of the rent taken in by these landlords is pure profit. Lewis Rudin, one of the great real estate legends of the twentieth century, once advised, "Never sell, keep debt low, and stay liquid."

The theory here is that you shouldn't sell an income-producing investment. Eventually, after it's paid for in full, it will still remain an income source. This can ultimately lead to wealth. I suppose this theory works better after you've gotten past the first investment. Many of the pitfalls of real estate investing occur when you're first getting started. A common problem is dealing with a loony tenant who tries to hold you responsible for every little thing, including items that may not actually be your responsibility. Once you're a wealthier investor, perhaps you can outsource management issues to somebody else. For the time being, you might have to take the hands-on approach and deal with problems on your own. Remember, the pitfalls of being a landlord apply only if you're renting out your real estate. If you live in it, you're responsible only for yourself and those who live with you.

Taxes

Property taxes are a reality. If you live in a neighborhood with high property taxes, you're probably shocked at how much you pay. It may or may not cheer you up to learn that those valuable tax dollars go toward public schools and local improvements to the neighborhood. Many people bundle their property taxes into their mortgage payment for convenience and therefore don't always take notice of the expense.

Property taxes are the reason many retirees move to Virginia or North Carolina. It's quite difficult in a place like Long Island or Los Angeles to find a home with reasonably low property taxes. If you do, there may be some catch that is even worse than high taxes. Although homeowners should carefully consider property taxes before making a purchase, it's also important to consider the fact that many areas with high property taxes have witnessed excellent price appreciation in property values in the past 20 years.

Lack of Liquidity

I already mentioned lack of liquidity as a benefit of investing in real estate, but if you need to free up some cash in a hurry, liquidating a home can be a bit of a mess. I used to live near a guy who had to deal with a rather unfortunate situation. The time came when he needed to free up the money in his home to meet big payments, including tuition for his son and a business debt. Because he had planned on downsizing anyway, he put the home up for sale rather than taking out a home equity loan. A few days before the scheduled closing, the buyer backed out of the deal because of a change in a divorce settlement that would leave him struggling with the payments. Unfortunately, the seller wasn't aware that the sale was contingent upon a factor as volatile as a divorce settlement. Similarly, the buyer had no clue that the seller needed $20,000 in 30 days or would start defaulting on some very important payments. The seller was forced to lower the price $20,000 to find a buyer who would close within 30 days.

These kinds of stories are not uncommon. When I create net worth statements, such as the one discussed in Chapter 2, the issue of home valuation comes up fairly often. It's interesting to see how people assign astronomical values to their homes when planning their retirements. They use generous assumptions to make the planning process a bit easier. Although generous assumptions make my job easier, I tend to use more conservative figures. Why? Life has a way of throwing us surprises. If we use conservative figures, we'll be more likely to reach our retirement goals. If the figures aren't realistic, the client and planner are just fooling themselves.

Smart owners hold on to their primary homes for a while, giving the property a chance to appreciate and themselves time to pay down the principal. If you find someone in my neighbor's situation, making a low-ball offer on a home with the promise of a quick closing could land you a good deal.

These are some of the things to think about when buying real estate. Keep in mind that there are myriad potential ways to profit from real estate investments. The buy-and-hold philosophy is fairly conservative, but not the only way to play the market. The quick flip tends to be quite profitable when the real estate market is hot. This happened frequently in 2003 and 2004. Buyers would secure homes, often with little or no money down, and simply pay interest for a few months until flipping the home to a new buyer for a quick profit. The hope was to make a quick buck by taking possession of the property, but not have to make more than a few payments. This strategy proved to be more dangerous in 2006 when home prices flattened out. Also, certain mortgages, such as those requiring little or no money down, can be a dangerous trap. We'll talk more about that in the following chapter.

Other real estate investors prefer the fix-up method. This entails buying a property at a discount because it has some sort of problem. Perhaps the floors are cracked, the roof is leaking, and the backyard hasn't been touched in 10 years. It might cost you $20,000 to restore the house, but it could potentially add substantially more than that to the resale price. If you did three or four of these a year, you could make a living at it, as many people do. You'd need access to handy-men, cheap supplies, and good financing to practice this type of real estate. Some people chase after foreclosures because often homes will be sold at a steep discount when the banks want to get rid of excess inventory.

Having a decent credit score will help (for more on credit scores, review Chapter 5), along with buying your home when interest rates are fairly reasonable. The length, amount, and type (fixed or variable rate) of your mortgage will factor in as well. We will get down to the nitty-gritty on mortgages in the next chapter.

For More Information

On the blog front, there are plenty of honorable mentions in addition to the two tips already given. For a truly comprehensive blog that covers real estate, mortgages, and development news, check out www.therealestatebloggers.com. This is an excellent source of up-to-date real estate information. I also enjoy the blog at www.inman.com, a large, independent real estate web site and media news service. This blog is loaded with unique and relevant content.

If you're concerned about issues surrounding overheating in the real estate market, check out some of the bubble blogs. One such blog is http://housingdoom.com. This site is the creation of Debi Averett and John McLeod. They pull quotes and factoids from a variety of sources that discuss what is seen as the pending doom of the housing market. If you're in the Phoenix area, you'll get special attention.

HousingPANIC at http://housingpanic.blogspot.com is another favorite of mine. The blog generates a lot of interesting feedback and has funny visuals as well.

Web Hot Spots

www.thelandlordblog.com

www.curbed.com

www.therealestatebloggers.com

www.inman.com

http://housingdoom.com

http://housingpanic.blogspot.com

CHAPTER

19

How Can I Unravel the Mortgage Mystery?

I was recently speaking with a homeowner from New York about his feelings on the current real estate market. I suggested that paying rent for a year while observing the price fluctuations of new condo developments might not be such a bad idea. He commented that owning always makes more sense than renting because mortgages allow owners to "move money from their left pocket to their right pocket." I thought about this comment for a moment, and then explained why it wasn't nearly that simple. The reality is that for every dollar you pull out of your left pocket, a pile of change falls on the floor, and often only a few cents will make it into your right pocket. The floor, of course, represents the bank.

This person, like many others, is overlooking the potential impact of the interest that gets paid to the lender during the life of the mortgage. The bank, especially during the earliest years of a mortgage, often takes a huge bite out of your payment. In some cases, as we'll discuss later on, the mortgage could even *add* money onto the principal balance of the mortgage. The borrower's assumption, which has historically been reasonably safe, is that the home will appreciate in value enough to offset the costs of borrowing.

I'd like to give an example of a typical mortgage repayment schedule to illustrate how payments get divided between paying down principal and paying interest to the bank. If you take out a 30-year mortgage at a rate of 7 percent on a $300,000 property, not

145

including taxes, carrying costs, or anything else you can build into the monthly payment, you would owe roughly $2,000 each month. However, the first payment on that mortgage would apply only about $200 from your left pocket toward the principal (your right pocket) and $1,800 to the bank (your money falling onto the floor). It's not until the very late years of the mortgage that the large majority of payment is going toward paying down the principal.

Surprisingly, I've found that many people, homeowners included, don't understand how this process, known as amortization, works. This schedule generally benefits the lender, because most people don't stay in their homes for 30 years. They sell after 10 years when the bank has already maximized profit and is more than willing to unload the property and move on to more new borrowers.

What Should I Look For in a Mortgage?

More people than ever have taken out mortgages in the past 10 years. Lenders have stepped up marketing efforts with traditional mortgage products and have utilized more innovative products, such as the interest-only mortgage, to attract a wider base of customers. This is good in that more people than ever can purchase homes. It's dangerous in that some people who aren't quite ready to buy a home are making the purchase anyway. Here are my three most important tips for those considering borrowing funds to purchase property.

Take Out a Fixed-Rate Mortgage

It's not often that you'll hear me give absolute advice. Financial planning is very subjective, and generally speaking, what may be a good fit for one person isn't necessarily appropriate for another. That being said, I've witnessed too many people get burned with adjustable-rate mortgage (ARM) products they don't properly understand. We live in a world where consumers are impulsive and producers are often looking for a profit regardless of moral reprehensibility. As a result of this dangerous interplay, consumers jump on offers that look appealing but where the fine print will have them paying through their teeth later on.

A fixed-rate mortgage will give you firm numbers you can rely on and factor into your budget. You won't have to figure out what the new payment is each month, or think about loans that reset, or possibly vary based on unpredictable economic factors such as interest-rate cycles and the words of the Federal Reserve policy makers.

Put 20 Percent Down on Your Home

A traditional mortgage will often require somewhere between 10 percent and 25 percent as a down payment. This amount acts as a safety net for both the buyer and the lender. First, it gives the buyer some equity protection against price volatility. If you buy a house without putting any money down and for some reason need to sell it after one year, you may run into a problem. If the home price dips 5 percent in that year and your broker charges another 5 percent to execute the sale, you could find yourself losing $50,000 fairly quickly on a $500,000 home purchase. The down payment tends to ensure that the buyer not get trapped in a situation in which negative equity could arise. It also provides peace of mind to the lender in that you've dedicated a substantial chunk of capital to the home purchase and will, it is hoped, be less likely to default on your mortgage obligation.

Second, your monthly payment is smaller with a larger down payment. If you recall our earlier example, the buyer is paying back a lot of interest on each borrowed dollar. Each extra dollar the buyer can scrape together for the down payment will reduce the amount of principal and, more important, the amount of interest that eventually gets repaid on the loan. There probably are people who would disagree with me about making larger down payments, namely experienced borrowers who have been successful at utilizing the maximum amount of leverage they can obtain. These people could argue that a smaller down payment will allow the borrower to keep more cash on hand (liquidity) while gaining the same amount of exposure to the property. In theory, the smaller down payment would accomplish the goal, assuming the property appreciates at a respectable rate. In this regard, I suppose my advice is conservative. Nonetheless, *truly* conservative people would probably be looking to put 50 percent or even 100 percent down on the home and would be much more cautious about what they borrow. I've found that in a majority of situations, especially with primary residences, 20 percent should be the minimum down payment.

Third, with a 20 percent down payment, you probably won't have to pay private mortgage insurance (PMI). This insurance, which is typically factored into the loan, protects the bank in the event that you default. It costs somewhere in the ballpark of 1 percent of the loan amount and is extremely difficult to avoid. The large down payment provides the bank with some assurance as to your qualifications as a buyer and releases you from this liability.

The fourth reason, perhaps the most important, is psychological in nature. Putting together a 20 percent down payment is not easy for most people. They will learn many lessons about spending and saving in the process of gathering $100,000. This will very possibly lead to more responsible habits and a better understanding of the costs associated with home ownership. This thought process is understood by the banks and building managers, who often require large down payments to prevent excessive default rates.

When Possible, Take Out a Shorter-Term Mortgage

A shorter-term mortgage has two huge potential advantages. The first is that a larger percentage of your payment goes toward the repayment of principal rather than interest to the bank. This could be construed as a different spin on the concept of increasing your down payment. The other advantage is that the interest rates are generally lower on shorter-term mortgages. This equates to more money for you and less money for the bank. Something else to think about: You'll be done making payments a lot faster!

As a rule of thumb in financial planning, we estimate that your mortgage payment should represent approximately a third of your net income. In other words, if your take-home pay is $100,000 per year, you should be spending roughly $33,000 each year on mortgage costs. With a 15-year mortgage at a rate of 6 percent, this would allow you to borrow about $330,000 and remain within your budgeting boundaries.

Which Is Better, a Fixed-Rate or an Adjustable-Rate Mortgage?

You may have noticed my preference for fixed-rate mortgages based on my earlier advice. Having said that, one of the early decisions one must make when getting started on the mortgage process is whether a fixed-rate or an adjustable-rate mortgage (ARM) makes more sense for the individual. The fixed-rate mortgage is fairly straightforward: The borrower makes the same payment, based on the same rate of interest, throughout the length of the loan. The monthly amount will always be roughly the same, but the portions of each payment that go toward interest and principal, which we discussed earlier, will change. Generally, payments during the earlier years will consist primarily of interest, whereas in the later years they will pay more principal. You can ask your lender for an amortization schedule to view these details of the payment structure.

 Tip: Payments on a fixed-rate mortgage become effectively smaller through time because of inflation. Consider the value of a $1,000 mortgage payment that began in 1987. That payment, which may have stung at the time, probably wouldn't seem so bad today.

Among the factors that will affect a borrower with a fixed mortgage product are the length of the loan and the current interest rate environment. Interest rates in the economy vary based on a variety of factors. I won't get into detail about this here but I will discuss the economy and the Federal Reserve in Chapter 23. The rate you obtain on a fixed mortgage is some combination of economic forces, the details of your loan, and your personal credibility, generally measured by your credit score. Lower rates are awarded to borrowers with clean credit, high incomes, and sizable down payments. If interest rates are low, as they were back in 2002 and 2003, the fixed-rate mortgage may be very appealing. If interest rates are high, as they were in parts of the 1980s, you may not feel so good about locking in a 12 percent rate.

You'll also typically get a better rate on a five- or seven-year mortgage than you will going out 20 or 30 years. Short-term loans are generally considered less risky and more predictable than long-term loans, although this not an exact science. Economic cycles do factor into these rates, and it's possible that rates on a long-term mortgage could be lower than those for a shorter-term one. This may be the result of an inverted yield curve—an economic phenomenon that generally, although not always, precedes an economic slowdown.

The interest rate paid on an adjustable-rate mortgage will vary over time. Initially, the borrower pays a rate that is often lower than most fixed-rate alternatives. However, the rate on the adjustable loan will reset based on a table arranged between the borrower and the lender. Typically, adjustable-rate loans will reset after one, three, five, or ten years. Both the borrower and the lender take on certain risks as to whether rates will be higher or lower in the future when the rates adjust.

While some people are naturally inclined to lock in their low rate for five or ten years, the trade-off could be an even lower interest rate if they agree to a reset after one or three years. You see, there is no right or wrong answer about this. Those willing to subject themselves to frequent readjustments will often be rewarded with the most competitive rates. Typically, the earlier years of ARMs will provide the lowest payments and the later years will become more expensive. Again, some of these terms are negotiable and will be decided upon before the first payment.

The interest-only mortgage is the ultimate form of lending flexibility. This option became quite popular in 2003 and 2004, when the housing boom was in full effect. The idea of paying nothing but interest is quite appealing to people who want to maximize the amount of house they can live in without maximizing the payments. There are a few situations in which this product can be very beneficial. For example, if you're planning on staying five years or less in your new home, the interest-only option may provide you with the lowest possible payments during your stay. You won't pay down any principal on the property, but your monthly outlay will be controllable. Another example would be a person who wants to move into a larger home but can't comfortably afford to pay for it. If the borrower is expecting either a pay raise or a new source of income within the next few years, the interest-only option will reduce the payment in the short run and can then be adjusted when the borrower has enough money to start paying down principal.

Sounds pretty cool, right? I've seen some interest-only payments on a $500,000 mortgage that ran only about $2,500 per month. However, very rarely do I see these products being used for the right reasons. Rather, speculators and homeowners who are trying to keep pace with the Jones family next door have been utilizing this product. The problem is that not everybody fully understands the future risks. Plenty of people who took out these mortgages in 2003 and 2004 are in the process of having their interest rates reset. The new payment is based on some new, potentially higher interest rates or the addition of principal into the payment, or both. Since rates have risen substantially since 2003, many of these payments are doubling. If the homeowner got used to a low payment and didn't plan properly for the payment increase, there could be a disaster. In some cases, homeowners will be forced to leave their homes, often with little or no equity in them at all. If by chance the value of housing doesn't keep up, this can present a negative equity situation such as the one mentioned earlier. The point is to be careful about interest-only mortgages and do your homework before you take one out.

What Is the Value of a Mortgage Broker?

Some people ask me if they should take out a mortgage directly from their bank. It seems logical, since banks lend money and the loan officer who can answer all your questions is probably only 10 steps away. The alternative is using a mortgage broker, who may have relationships with multiple banks and can talk you through the lending process. My experience has shown that mortgage brokers do typically add some value into the mortgage process. The increased competition they cause in the industry tends to keep the cost of borrowing somewhat more reasonable. A mortgage broker can add even more value to a person with less than perfect credit who might have trouble obtaining competitive mortgage rates and would need to shop around a lot before signing up. Mortgage brokers can also translate the long contracts and financial jargon you will inevitably encounter into simple English.

I'd recommend speaking with the loan officer at your bank in addition to a mortgage broker. You may as well keep both options open to see where you can find the best deals.

The Bottom Line

As a passionate investor, I understand that real estate equity will ultimately represent the majority of wealth obtained by millions of Americans. The concept of borrowing money to buy a home, traditionally through a mortgage, will allow people to secure real estate that would otherwise be too expensive. For middle-income citizens, mortgages will continue to drive the incredible rates of home ownership we experience here in the United States. Further, as I mentioned in the previous chapter, the equity in one's home will often represent a crucial nest egg during retirement.

My approach to financing a home purchase is based on my own experiences with people who have been through the ups and downs of paying for a home. Remember, the same fine print that allows you to secure a mortgage can cause you to lose it. By taking a conservative approach, you can protect yourself against many potential risks. Plan carefully, and be honest with your finances. This approach will ultimately reward you.

For More Information

If you're looking for interesting mortgage news with links to other mortgage and real estate resources, visit www.mortgageblog.com. Whenever I drop in at this blog, the articles are timely and appealing to a broad range of readers. There's also an interesting blog in the mortgage section of www.bankrate.com. It deals with how mortgages and real estate are affected by economic factors. Needless to say, lots of useful information about mortgages can be found on the Bankrate. com site. To find all the Bankrate blogs, just use the search box on the upper right side of the screen.

If you want to expose yourself to the dark side of mortgages, visit www.mortgagefraudblog.com. This site is run by Rachel Dollar, a mortgage broker and attorney in California. She has recently become quite the authority on collecting and organizing fraudulent activity in the world of mortgages and exposing it on the Web. Reading about fraud and the various protections available for consumers can teach you a lot about how the process works.

Web Hot Spots

www.mortgageblog.com

www.bankrate.com

www.mortgagefraudblog.com

CHAPTER 20

What Are All These Different Financial Designations?

Have you ever been confused by a designation printed on a business card? Perhaps it said "John Stern, ChFC." Well, that's excellent for Mr. Stern, and I'm thrilled to see he has furthered his education, but what exactly does that mean? What good does a designation do for clients or consumers if they don't know what it represents? More important, how is a consumer to distinguish those designations that are difficult to obtain from those that exist more to dress up a business card or practice? For example, Wealth Management Specialist (WMS) and Certified Financial Planner (CFP) are both financial planning designations. However, becoming a WMS can be done through self-study and without the burden of continuing education requirements. Becoming a CFP involves a two-day, 10-hour examination, along with rigorous experience and continuing education requirements, and there is a strict code of ethics to boot. Which professional would you rather work with?

As I continue investigating my own credentials as a financial adviser, I'm regularly learning new and interesting facts about how the designation business really works. The reason I say business, rather than process, is to clear up any misconception that designations exist purely for the benefit of consumers. Issuing organizations make money as well, generally through membership fees and costs associated with study guides, classroom sessions, examinations, and continuing education. That's not to suggest issuing organizations don't deserve to earn a profit—they most certainly do—but as we always say in finance, "disclosure, disclosure, disclosure." The issuing organization, especially if it is a for-profit entity, should take responsibility for explaining the need for the designation in the industry and how the organization makes money.

It should also be clear that a professional who maintains an armament of designations isn't necessarily better suited for your needs. There is usually a correlation between designations and experience, but ultimately the decision about who to work with, especially when it comes to your money, is a more personal issue. The concept of designations is analogous to the degrees conferred by our education system in the United States. One might think that obtaining a bachelor's degree from an Ivy League university necessarily indicates a better education, more career opportunities, and higher earnings potential. Statistically, this is still probably true; however, this is not an exact science in the world we live in. With billionaires lacking college diplomas and Ivy League graduates searching for jobs, we have to rethink our traditional assumptions. Similarly, having multiple designations may indicate that somebody is better qualified to advise, but not that he or she is necessarily a better choice to advise *you*.

Which Designations Should I Look Out For?

First I'll describe what I refer to as the "big three." These are, in my opinion, the most significant financial credentials in terms of recognition and popularity. Then I'll go into a discussion of some other notable designations, many of which are new and may become more prevalent in the future. If you come across some letters that aren't mentioned here and you're unfamiliar with them, do some quick research on the Web. There are way too many financial designations for me to break them all down. Or you could go right to http://apps.nasd.com/datadirectory/nasd/prodesignations .aspx, a web page of the National Association of Securities Dealers (NASD) that can break down most financial designations in just a few seconds.

- *Chartered Financial Analyst (CFA).* This designation, issued by the CFA Institute (www.cfainstitute.org), is among the more difficult designations that a financial services professional can obtain. It also appeals to a very specific group of people. The process requires a lot of course work and generally takes a couple of years to complete. The candidate must demonstrate knowledge in securities analysis, accounting, economics, and investments. A CFA should have a decent advantage when it comes to getting a job in the securities, portfolio management, and financial advising industries because of the experience it necessitates. In fact, only 36 percent of applicants who sat for the CFA exam in 2005 passed the first round of testing.*

- *Certified public accountant (CPA).* The CPA is a state-issued designation for people who wish to become accountants. Automatically, you can assume a certain degree of credibility when it comes to state-issued letters. Like the CFA, sitting for the CPA exams requires a bachelor's degree from an accredited university. In addition, CPA candidates are required to have experience in the industry and pass a series of exams (which I've heard are quite difficult) administered by the state board of accountancy. There are ethical standards to adhere to and continuing education requirements to ensure that you stay up-to-date with news and changes in the industry that could affect you and/or your clients.

- *Certified Financial Planner (CFP).* The CFP designation was created specifically for the financial planning profession. It is issued by the Certified Financial Planner Board of Standards (www.cfp.net), and the qualifying examination is offered only upon completion of a series of modules that cover over a hundred financial planning topics. A major part of holding this designation is adhering to the CFP Board's "Code of Ethics and Professional Responsibility." Naturally, financial professionals are held to the highest standard of ethics because of the importance of the responsibility they undertake. It's no secret that people are very protective of their money.

So, we have the three designations that are more or less household names. Then, we have a variety of other designations, which range in specialty and purpose. When it comes to financial planning designations, there is a lot of material overlap. For example,

---

*www.cfainstitute.org/pressroom/05releases/20050818_01.html.

Chartered Financial Consultant (ChFC) has considerable overlap with CFP, but the ChFC is issued by the American College (www.theamericancollege.edu), and the CFP is issued by the Certified Financial Planner Board of Standards. Overlap is actually a good thing in the designation business because it encourages higher standards and steeper competition over being the "authority" designation. Perception is obviously a big factor when you're in the designation business. In the world of financial planning, here are some letters that you may see floating around:

- *Chartered Financial Consultant (ChFC)*. The ChFC has considerable overlap with the Certified Financial Planner designation. It's my impression that somebody with a CFP would probably not consider getting the ChFC an immediate priority. In fact, those with a ChFC automatically qualify to sit for the CFP exam. My feeling is that insurance professionals lean toward the ChFC for a broader knowledge on financial planning whereas new financial planners tend to sit directly for the CFP.
- *Chartered Life Underwriter (CLU)*. The CLU is an insurance designation. Its purpose is to ensure a high level of knowledge when dealing with life insurance. A financial planner who tends to do a lot of insurance business may consider obtaining this designation as a standout credential. The CLU, like the ChFC, is issued by the American College.
- *Certified Senior Advisor (CSA)*. This designation is aimed to educate financial professionals on the issues that are of specific importance to older folk. It is one of several designations that exist to deal with social, health-related, and financial issues faced by seniors. While I like this designation for what it represents, it doesn't have the sort of experience requirements that I generally look for in financial designations. The issuing organization, the Society of Certified Senior Advisors (www.society-csa.com), is really the first I've seen to fully integrate health issues into the financial planning process. While that may sound logical, it's quite impressive in that it brings another level of knowledge and communication to an already complex process.

The senior market is indeed one that doesn't get all the attention it deserves. Considering the aging population and increasing life expectancies, I fully advocate more focus on elder care and a better general understanding of insurance policies that may be essential. The AARP (www.aarp.org) is a leading advocacy group dedicated to people over age 50. It offers resources such as product discounts for members, discussions about legislation that could affect the senior market, and one of the nation's most popular newsletters, mulling over issues such as Social Security and Medicare.

In 2006, a new designation that I consider to be quite note-worthy made its debut. It's the Qualified Plan Financial Consultant (QPFC) designation, sponsored by the American Society of Pension Professionals & Actuaries (www.asppa.org). This new designation was launched at the 2006 401(k) summit in Orlando, Florida. The purpose is to further educate investment professionals who specialize in qualified plan sales and consulting. Qualified plans, for those who aren't familiar with the lingo, generally refer to retirement plans such as the 401(k) or 403(b) that receive favorable tax treatment as defined by the IRS tax code. I think this might be a successful designation because of the number of people invested in these sorts of plans who have questions about them. Receiving inaccurate advice about retirement plans can be a particularly costly and aggravating experience. If the QPFC mark takes off as planned, it could put some focus on this area of financial planning ahead of the first round of baby boomer retirements. Not only do the boomers stand to benefit from this mark, but corporate America, which is rapidly transitioning to defined-contribution plans such as the 401(k) and 403(b), will stand to benefit from this improved knowledge as well.

Also gaining in popularity is the Chartered Alternative Investment Analyst (CAIA) designation launched back in 2003 by the Chartered Alternative Investment Analyst Association (www.caia.org). In the past few years, the overall flow of investment funds has been particularly friendly toward hedge funds, private equity, managed futures, and commodities. If some readers are not familiar with the fundamentals of these investment styles, this is probably partly because of the complexity involved with these investments and partly because of the fact that they target the high-net-worth market. The latter reason is actually changing, though, and I think future evolution of the investment industry may allow middle-class investors to get their feet wet with alternative investments as well. This CAIA designation is unique in that it educates a widening group of financial professionals to help them better serve the needs of an evolving client base.

What Should I Make of Designations I Haven't Heard Of?

You may have questions about a lesser-known designation or a newer one that hasn't received a ton of publicity. As a general rule, I try to give the benefit of the doubt to professionals who meet the requirements for a new designation, even if it's not the most rigorous choice. At the very least, the candidate is making an effort to further his or her knowledge and stay focused on industry issues. Fortunately, there are some fairly easy ways to form conclusions about designations and the professionals who use them. For example, those who seek out credentials that require little or no continuing education are most likely in search of quick letters that won't haunt them with overly burdensome requirements in the future. In contrast, those who sit for the CFP or ChFC are making a statement about their career ambitions. Similarly, a designation that can be earned through self-study and an exam taken on your home computer might garner less respect from other financial professionals.

For me, the most important issue is the public's lack of understanding when it comes to financial designations and their requirements. This can lead to misunderstandings, such as someone presenting easy-to-obtain letters as decisive credentials. Furthermore, I'm sure the CFP who learned over a hundred topics and sat for a 10-hour exam would find that highly unfair. Another interesting question here is whether the investigative burden should lie with the issuing organization, the financial professional, or the consumer. I think it's fair to say that consumers should not be fully expected to navigate through an industry with which they are unfamiliar. The issuing organization is more or less free of blame because it can't force people into sitting for its letters; it can just market them and hope that they receive some form of recognition. I would say that, in most cases, it is the financial professionals who should be held responsible for how they present themselves and their credentials to the public. We live in a world of increasing attention to corporate governance, where we are constantly on the lookout for the sake of the little investor. Any misrepresentation that affords an advantage to a financial professional will be looked down upon and will, one hopes, be short-lived.

The Bottom Line

There are a few things you should take away from this discussion. The first is that designations really do matter. *Most* of the time, an adviser with more professional designations will be better qualified to serve you. Working with a Series 7 licensed stockbroker is not the same as working with a financial adviser armed with a CFA and a CFP. As a consumer, you should take home that business card and verify the legitimacy of those letters. Use the NASD link mentioned above to demystify a host of different financial designations. It discloses information about the issuing organization, the examination requirements, how one would study for the exam, and what the continuing education requirements are.

Web Hot Spots

http://apps.nasd.com/datadirectory/nasd/prodesignations .aspx

www.cfainstitute.org

www.cfp.net

www.theamericancollege.edu

www.society-csa.com

www.aarp.org

www.asppa.org

www.caia.org

CHAPTER

21

Exploring the Variable Annuity: What's All the Chatter About?

The chatter surrounding variable annuities is louder than ever. Investors want security regarding their money in the face of increasing amounts of uncertainty about the future. Variable annuities may provide this security through two features not generally offered together: the opportunity for growth combined with a variety of guarantees protecting both the payment to a beneficiary if the account owner dies and the income derived from the principal amount invested.

What differentiates an annuity from, say, a mutual fund investment is that an insurance company can actually offer guarantees. The investment sales community, especially in light of a recent increase in disclosure requirements, must be careful about promising things to clients that they can't provide. Having a guarantee to cover one's principal investment, and possibly the income derived from it, is extremely appealing. In a sense, it can act as a substitute for the pension some may hope for but never see. If you don't have a pension, the annuity will let you turn your own lump-sum investment into a customizable stream of income with a reasonable sense of security.

As with most concepts that sound too good to be true, annuities have their flaws. They are often criticized for being expensive, not always justifying their costs, and being too heavily marketed. I don't take a hard stance in favor of or against the variable annuity as an investment product. I think for some people it's a great option, and for others (generally those with a solid background in investing) it's probably not the best choice. I prefer to put all the facts on the table and let you form your own opinion about the variable annuity.

What Are the Features of a Variable Annuity?

An annuity is a stream of income. An investor can make either a lump-sum purchase or periodic purchase payments during the accumulation phase of an annuity. At some point, the total value of the annuity (purchases plus investment gains) can be exchanged for a schedule of payments with a variety of different guarantees. The investor can usually customize to some degree the terms of the contract.

What makes an annuity variable is the fluctuating performance of the subaccounts in which it invests. Typically, annuity subaccounts are invested in portfolios of stocks and bonds. The total contract value of your annuity will vary depending on the performance of the underlying subaccounts. Obviously, some annuities will offer better investment options than others. This is something to consider in an annuity for you. I've often found that multimanager platforms—investment options that include popular sub-accounts from a variety of investment companies—are an appealing feature.

Because annuities are issued by insurance companies, Congress allows them to grow tax-deferred under current tax laws. This tax deferral allows appreciation and interest to grow free of income tax until withdrawn from the contract. This is similar to other retirement plans such as the 401(k) that offer tax deferral as well. Because annuities are often retirement-oriented, long-term investment vehicles, the account owner may have to pay a 10 percent IRS penalty on any money withdrawn prior to age 59½.

The insurance aspect includes any single guarantee or combination of guarantees available from the service provider. There are often additional riders that can be purchased to spice up the contract as well. Many annuity providers continuously update the insurance features in an effort to give themselves an advantage over rival service providers. The death benefit and the guaranteed minimum income benefit (GMIB) are two of the more popular features offered on today's contracts.

Death Benefit

The death benefit is a fairly standard feature of most variable annuities. The insurance company will make a payment to a spouse or other named beneficiary if the annuity holder dies. The beneficiary will generally receive the greater of either the account balance at the time of death *or* whatever the initial investment was, less any withdrawals taken. For example, if you invest $100,000 in 2002, which grows to $150,000 before you die, your beneficiary would get $150,000. If the markets had a sour decade and the contract was worth only $75,000 at the time of death, the beneficiary would still get the initial $100,000, assuming no withdrawals had been taken.

Some service providers offer a stepped-up death benefit. This feature, often referred to as a "ratchet," will allow the contract to be upwardly adjusted every few years to lock in market gains. If the new market value is higher, the death benefit and possibly the income stream derived from it will benefit from the increase. This further entices investors by allowing the guarantee of a higher beneficiary payout, even if the market turns sour the year after the ratchet. Naturally, this sort of benefit will cost you in the form of higher expenses. Certain limits may apply with these sorts of benefits, so you'll want to read the contract carefully.

Guaranteed Minimum Income Benefit

If you decide to annuitize your purchase payments into a stream of income, you'll have to choose a period of time over which to receive your payout. It can be a fixed number of years, such as 10, or it can be for life. The GMIB guarantees that the annuitant will receive a certain minimum amount of income while alive. The insurance company runs the risk that the account owner could live to a ripe old age, resulting in a possible loss of money on that contract. However, insurance companies are pretty darn smart. They understand that the majority of account owners will die somewhere within the standard mortality tables.

This income guarantee comes in a few different flavors. Sometimes the guarantee is on the accumulation amount. Other times it is on the withdrawal amount. However you phrase it, the objectives are fairly similar. The contract will provide some form of certainty regarding the possibility that your account doesn't grow fast enough to support your payments. The minimum payment is usually either a percentage of the account value or a percentage of the stepped-up account value, regardless of how the underlying investments have performed. The guaranteed minimum withdrawal benefit (GMWB) has been particularly popular because it doesn't require the account owner to annuitize the account and give up that aspect of control. The account owner can withdraw a certain percentage of the account each year, usually until the entire value has been taken out.*

———————

These benefits—death benefit, GMIB, and GWIB—often work well with investors who are looking for growth combined with income. They can keep a growth-oriented asset allocation and remain confident about a certain minimum guaranteed level of income. Keep in mind that any of these additional guarantees regarding income, withdrawals, or accumulation will cost money. Investors should analyze these costs carefully to determine whether they are worth paying.

Criticisms of the Variable Annuity

As I've mentioned, there is considerable criticism over the variable annuity. Costs, surrender charges, and tax treatment are among the complaints that are frequently thrown around. There are also mounting concerns about the use of annuities in already tax-qualified plans such as the 401(k) and 403(b). Let's get into some of these complaints to see whether they are legitimate.

Costs

The costs of an annuity depend in part on which features and riders the annuity owner has selected. That being said, all variable annuities have mortality and expense (M&E) charges, which cover the insurance aspect of the contract. When combined with the expenses of the underlying investments, annuity expenses typically

———————

*Guarantees are based on the claims-paying ability of the issuer. Surrender charges may apply. Gains from tax-deferred investments are taxable as ordinary income upon withdrawal. The investment returns and principal value of the available sub-account portfolios will fluctuate so that the value of an investor's unit, when redeemed, may be worth more or less than their original value. Optional features may involve additional fees.

run 2 to 2.5 percent, while domestic mutual funds tend to hover around the 1 to 1.5 percent level.*

My feeling is that critics are mostly concerned about what, if any, value is really added by the features of an annuity. Are the insurance companies protecting consumers from real risks? Or do they simply use scare tactics to promote an investment product that lacks in value? For example, the death benefit is the primary feature of most annuity contracts, yet every few months I come across an article that accuses the death benefit of being superfluous. The argument is that there are few situations in which a long-term contract invested in stocks and bonds would decrease in value enough that the beneficiary would be better off taking the initial principal investment rather than the current contract value. If an investor considers the past perform-ance of the markets, this benefit affects only beneficiaries of those who purchase an annuity contract and die soon afterward. However, insurance companies generally put an age cap on who can buy their contracts, protecting them from extremely old people receiving too many guarantees.

If you really crunch the numbers, it'll be clear that insurance companies are not in the business of losing money to probability. That being said, they are in the business of providing certainty of income, or peace of mind. An annuity will usually offer you that, even if a hefty price tag is attached.

We could have a similar discussion about the guaranteed mini-mum income benefit as well, but the point is more or less the same. The GMIB could be criticized as primarily a peace-of-mind benefit that may not be cost-effective. This criticism would probably come more from a savvy investor or other person who studies probability the same way an actuary does.

Surrender Charges

Annuities, because they are designed to be long-term savings vehi-cles, often have steep withdrawal penalties. In the first several years of the contract, the owner is usually allowed to withdraw only a small

---

*According to Variable Annuity Research and Data Service, 2.148 percent is the average for variable annuity expenses as of March 31, 2006. Average mutual fund expenses are 1.32 percent, based on data as of June 30, 2006, compiled by Morningstar, Inc., of the average expense ratios of domestic equity, taxable bond, municipal bond, and foreign equity mutual funds.

percentage of the contract without penalty. Surrender charges vary but are usually on a descending scale from 6 or 7 percent down to 0 percent over 5 to 10 years.

Taxation of Earnings

Annuity benefits took a hit in 2003 when the long-term capital gains rate was reduced from 20 percent to 15 percent. Long-term capital gains (held for one year or more) are currently taxed at a maximum of 15 percent. However, investment earnings on annuities are taxed at the ordinary income bracket, which could be much higher. While the other benefits might still make the annuity worth it, this adds fuel to the arguments of the critics.

Annuities in Qualified Plans

Annuities also receive an increased level of criticism when offered in tax-qualified plans. The argument is that 401(k) and 403(b) plans already have tax-deferred status, and the increased costs of using the variable annuity will reduce the performance of the subaccounts over longer periods of time. Many think it's not worth using a variable annuity for this purpose.

In fact, the Securities and Exchange Commission (SEC)'s own web site highlights the fact that variable annuities offer no additional tax benefit to that of a 401(k) or an IRA (www.scc.gov/investor/pubs/varannty.htm). The SEC cautions that you should use the variable annuity in a 401(k) or IRA vehicle only if it makes sense because of the annuity's other features, such as lifetime income payments and death benefit protection.

I can sympathize with this criticism, as I've seen it in real life. While teaching, my mother participated in a 403(b) plan that was offered through a variable annuity platform. She had major problems transferring in and out of sub-accounts because of the surrender charges. She also found that the high costs were holding back the performance of her investments, especially during sideways markets. The problems were compounded by the fact that a low-cost mutual fund platform would have offered the same tax-deferred status at a lower cost. After doing some research, we were able to transfer her out of the variable annuity platform and into a lower-cost alternative.

The Bottom Line

This is the basic story with annuities. A true do-it-yourself investor could probably manually create a cheaper product by purchasing insurance contracts for the death benefit and having low-cost investments centered around bonds and dividend-paying stocks for the income stream. Plus, you wouldn't have to deal with any holding periods or surrender charges. Whereas it might ultimately be cheaper this way, it would require a certain degree of research and knowledge about what you want to sort through the various risks and choices.

Having dealt with the annuity question in my career, I can state that peace of mind is often what keeps clients interested in this type of product. I've noticed that the media often point to the commission paid to brokers and advisers as a reason for the surge in variable annuity sales. While it may be a factor, the decrease in pension benefits and government entitlements is more likely the primary driver in annuity popularity. The convenience (and comfort) of packaged products is definitely a factor as well. Justifying higher costs in the face of convenience to do-it-yourself investors is near impossible. If you have a good financial planner, especially one who works on a fee basis, he or she should be able to explain the attributes of the variable annuity in clear English for you.

For More Information

Blogs that deal exclusively with annuities aren't all that common. It took me only about 30 seconds to figure out why. Most bloggers are do-it-yourself investors who would be less likely to utilize the variable annuity product. Consequently, very few bloggers focus on it. Also, because annuities are a topic of increased scrutiny, many professionals choose to steer clear of them on their web sites.

The one excellent annuity blog that I can reference here can be found at www.annuityiq.com/blog. This blog is written by Scott Demonte, an annuity expert who comes from a long line of financial planners. His web site has a resource that analyzes different annuities and helps you understand the differences between each. Besides that, his web site has loads of other good information.

For basic information about investment products, including various types of annuities, I like to reference Investopedia (www.investopedia.com) and the Motley Fool (www.fool.com). They are both safe bets in terms of reliable information.

The National Association of Securities Dealers (NASD) has its own investor education resource where you can learn about investment products. It can be found at www.saveandinvest.org. You can also learn about annuities and some of their potential drawbacks at the Securities and Exchange Commission (SEC)'s web site, located at www.sec.gov/investor/pubs/varannty.htm.

Web Hot Spots

www.annuityiq.com/blog

www.investopedia.com

www.fool.com

www.saveandinvest.org

www.sec.gov/investor/pubs/varannty.htm

PART

IV

THINKING LONG-TERM ABOUT MONEY MANAGEMENT

CHAPTER

22

How Can I Manage My Portfolio through Asset Allocation and Rebalancing?

At this point we've reviewed a variety of investment ideas, ranging from individual stocks to real estate. What we haven't discussed is how to manage a financial portfolio *after* it's put to work. Many financial professionals believe that the methods used to manage portfolios, including asset allocation and rebalancing strategies, will ultimately be the driving force of investment returns. In the long run, disciplined management could matter even more than which individual stocks and bonds you decide to include in your portfolio.*

What Is Asset Allocation?

Asset allocation is the process of distributing a portfolio over various asset classes. There are actually *two* schools of thought regarding asset allocation—strategic and tactical—and their objectives are quite different. Our primary focus will be on the strategic model because it highlights an investor's tolerance for risk using normal asset classes over the long run.

Tactical asset allocation, unlike strategic asset allocation, attempts to feel out economic inefficiencies that might cause one asset class to outperform another. An example might be allocating heavily into stocks

---

*Asset allocation strategies do not ensure a profit or protect against loss in declining markets.

after a terrorist attack causes a broad decline in stock prices that is believed to be temporary. Tactical asset allocation is interesting but often criticized for "market timing," defined as the attempt to predict the future direction of a market. Tactical asset allocation tends to appeal more to active investors with an appetite for risk.

When creating your asset allocation strategy, you should remember that your age will likely impact your tolerance for risk. Young people, with many years of earning potential ahead of them, can typically tolerate more volatility in their portfolios. Older investors, specifically those approaching retirement, have fewer potential years of earnings ahead of them and will therefore often allocate out of stocks and into bonds and other more conservative asset classes. Figure 22.1 is an example of what conservative, moderate, and aggressive asset allocations might look like.

 Note: This sample asset allocation model is for illustrative purposes only and does not represent a specific investment. Investors should meet with their financial representatives to discuss personal risk tolerance and suitable recommendations.

To illustrate the importance of asset allocation, take the example of Mr. Money, a 57-year-old planning on retiring at age 60 with $800,000 in his investment accounts. He currently has $700,000 in a portfolio, which is 75 percent stocks and 25 percent bonds. If we leave the portfolio as is, our expected rate of return would remain at 8 percent, the average return achieved by Mr. Money for the past 10 years. This rate of return, assuming all interest and capital gains were reinvested in the accounts, would easily get us past the $800,000 goal. In fact, it would leave Mr. Money with $881,798.

However, let's say the stock portion of the portfolio loses 10 percent over the following three years instead. The 25 percent invested in bonds would improve the return a little bit, but Mr. Money would still fall considerably short of his goal. He would reach age 60 with less than the $700,000 he currently has. This could possibly require him to push back retirement by a few more years or work part-time well into his 60s.

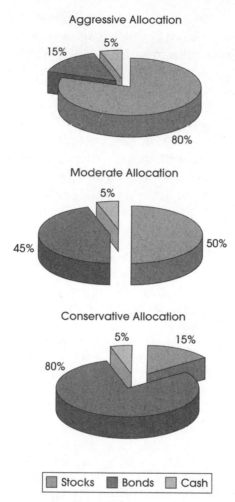

Aggressive Allocation

Moderate Allocation

Conservative Allocation

| Stocks | Bonds | Cash |

Figure 22.1 Basic Asset Allocations

Now, let's consider how using a smart asset allocation could avoid the idea of a retirement shortfall completely. What if Mr. Money allocated 100 percent of his money into bonds at age 57 instead? This would eliminate any risks that are specific to stocks. It would also reduce his overall level of volatility and create a reliable income steam. This would lower his expected rate of return to 5 percent, but provide much more peace of mind. His portfolio would presumably grow to $810,338 by age 60, meeting his retirement goal.

The example is pretty clear: Decisions about how much money to allocate into each asset class are about more than just which asset class has the highest expected return.

There is one other important consideration that puts a spin on this process: While it may be logical using past performance statistics to justify heavy allocations into stocks at a young age, many young people aren't comfortable with risk. The reason is often that they have substantially less money to invest than the average 40- or 50-year-old. This leads to certain protective feelings over their funds, which translate to higher allocations for savings and money market accounts, even if they aren't the best choices for growth.

Similarly, although less frequently, some older investors are bored by fixed-income investments and prefer to be more speculative, even if it's not the textbook thing to do. This tends to happen during long bull markets when it seems like every investment is lucrative. Any seasoned professional will understand that this is not the case and try to bring the asset allocation discussion back into play.

Which Asset Classes Should Be Included in an Investment Portfolio?

Although the financial markets have undergone an evolution recently in terms of investment vehicles that are available, most of them are slicing and dicing the same three asset classes: stocks, bonds, and cash/cash equivalents. Investing 100 percent in stocks, regardless of how you categorize them, will be the most aggressive scenario, and usually the one with the highest expected return.

An allocation of 100 percent in cash or money market instruments is the most conservative option, with a low expected rate of return but very little volatility within the portfolio. Some money market instruments, such as Treasury bills, offer a guaranteed rate of return that gives the investor a high degree of predictability. Needless to say, having 50 percent of your money in stocks and 50 percent in cash or fixed-income products will provide an opportunity for growth while maintaining a certain degree of stability.

Some people are further convinced that buying shares of companies that are oriented toward either growth or value can make a difference as well. There are various theories on each, but again, creating a strategy for your portfolio and sticking to your allocations will ultimately be more important than an orientation toward either growth or value.

What Is Portfolio Rebalancing?

Rebalancing is the idea of bringing a portfolio back to its target allocation after it starts to deviate. The deviation is quite natural, and is often a good thing. Consider the example of a $100,000 portfolio with 50 percent stocks and 50 percent bonds. If the stock market has a 20 percent return in a given year and the bond market returns 10 percent, you've now got $60,000 in stocks and $55,000 in bonds. Well done. You've made money. The only problem is that your risk tolerance, requiring a 50 percent split between stocks and bonds, is no longer accurate. However, if you took $2,500 out of the stock portion and put it in the bond portion, you would now have $57,500 in each. This is portfolio rebalancing. There are a bunch of reasons why this practice is encouraged:

- Rebalancing helps to mitigate risk by bringing the portfolio back to a target asset allocation. If our risk tolerance has changed, it gives us an opportunity to think about that as well.
- Rebalancing forces us to reduce our positions in assets that are outperforming and increase our positions in assets that are underperforming. This is an ideal situation for the average investor who doesn't monitor his portfolio to take profits and losses from time to time.
- Volatility is smoothed out with a careful rebalancing schedule. If we review the past performance of major indexes, we'd see sharp increases and sharp decreases in certain asset classes over time. Rebalancing creates the opportunity to benefit from these potential inefficiencies.

How Often Should I Rebalance?

This is a great question. I'd volunteer four times a year (quarterly) if it had to be a certain number of times per year, although the ideal answer would probably be when there is a percentage deviation from the desired allocation. Rebalancing each time the portfolio moves 5 percent from the target is perhaps a good rule of thumb. Rebalancing should be about keeping a certain mix of assets, not how much time has passed between updates.

At a more technical level, the frequency of rebalancing should be the result of the underlying volatility within the assets. If the assets are very volatile, rebalancing will be more important. If the assets have similar correlations, you probably won't find much need to rebalance because it will take longer for deviations to occur.

If your portfolio is full of assets with varying degrees of correlation (as a good portfolio generally should be) rebalancing will be much more effective than in a portfolio where all the assets move together.

Dollar Cost Averaging

This is an investment strategy utilized by people who either don't have a lump sum to invest or feel uncomfortable about letting all their money hit the market at the same time. The fear is very logical. What if I invest $25,000 today and tomorrow the market drops 5 percent? I've just lost $1,250 overnight. While this scenario is unlikely, it is possible. As an alternative, I can divide that $25,000 into 12 equal payments and make them on the first of each month. This way, the average cost per share could be lower if the market moves up gradually from your first purchase payment to your last. Also, any possibility of bad timing will be minimized.*

I happen to like dollar cost averaging. I think it's an easy concept to grasp and works well with many investor profiles. That being said, studies of the effectiveness of dollar cost averaging in terms of improving investment results are quite mixed. Many show that investing a lump sum works out to be smarter (more profitable) over the long run. This conclusion is also quite logical. Because the stock market has moved up slowly and somewhat steadily for the past 100 years, having a lump sum invested (more money up front) rather than utilizing dollar cost averaging (less money up front) would prove more effective. There are limited examples, such as the day before a market crash, in which a lump-sum investment turns out to be a bad idea.

That being said, logic is not the only factor that goes into investing. Since the longer-term investment results of implementing a dollar cost averaging strategy are only slightly lower than using a lump sum, some people still prefer to use the dollar cost averaging method. Whoever says that psychology and emotion

---

*Such a plan involves continuous investment in securities regardless of fluctuation in price levels of such securities. An investor should consider one's ability to continue purchasing through periods of low price levels. It does not ensure a profit and does not protect against loss in declining markets.

aren't part of the investment process doesn't know what he's talking about. It's half the battle. Whether or not it should be is a different and, quite frankly, less important discussion.

For More Information

There are plenty of blogs that deal with portfolio management issues, including asset allocation, rebalancing, and dollar cost averaging. You might want to drop in at http://abnormalreturns.com. Here you will find thoughts and opinions aimed at helping investors achieve abnormal (excess) returns without reading random market predictions. You'll also notice the site does a great job of linking to recent stories in newspapers and magazines, along with other blogs.

I'm also a fan of the Aleph Blog, found at http://alephblog.com. This blog is run by David Merkel, a leading commentator at www.realmoney.com. His overall focus is on portfolio management issues and strategies. David often comments on risk tolerance and has a category earmarked for asset allocation issues.

The Securities and Exchange Commission (SEC), the regulatory body that oversees the securities industry, also has an excellent resource run by its own Office of Investor Education and Assistance. It can be found at www.sec.gov/investor.shtml. The search box you will find can guide you to educational articles on asset allocation, rebalancing, and most other investment issues. In a sense, this is the ultimate reference site because the organization exists primarily to protect the interests of individual investors.

Web Hot Spots

http://abnormalreturns.com
http://alphablog.com
www.sec.gov/investor.shtml

CHAPTER 23

The Fed? Interest Rates? Inflation? Why Should I Care?

People often take for granted how efficient the U.S. economy is. One organization that contributes to this, whether or not consumers realize it, is the Federal Reserve Bank (www.federalreserve.gov). Commonly known as the Fed, this quasi-governmental agency has three stated goals. In order of importance, they are: to keep the prices of goods and services relatively stable (prevent inflation), to maximize the number of people who are employed, and to moderate long-term interest rates. The third goal is sort of implied in that stable interest rates are a natural consequence of stable prices.

If you take a moment to consider the enormity of these tasks, it'll make the chapter more interesting. The Fed has a bunch of policy tools it can use to control the supply of money and help the economy reach these stated goals. I think understanding how these policy tools manifest themselves in the lives of consumers is just as important as knowing what these tools are. I wish somebody had added this discussion into my Economics 101 curriculum. It wasn't until I began watching CNBC religiously that I started connecting economic theory and practice in my head.

Why Do We Listen to the Fed?

Have you ever noticed how much buzz surrounds the policy decisions of the Federal Reserve Bank? It seems like any time the policy makers breathe, somebody is looking to analyze how it may impact the economy. This is not without reason—the Fed dominates the national banking system. All it needs to do is imply that a policy change may be necessary, and the market will adjust accordingly.

Without this organized banking system allowing for liquidity and lending, the economy could not have produced or supported the amount of wealth that it has. It would take many people their whole lives to save up enough cash to buy a home outright. Similarly, without banks involved, it would take much larger groups of investors to pool the money necessary to put up new office towers and residential complexes. An efficient banking system is crucial for any economy seeking expansion.

What Are These Tools?

The most common tool used by the Federal Reserve Bank to control the money supply is adjusting the federal funds rate, the overnight interest rate that banks charge each other to borrow money. When you hear on the news that "the Fed raised rates today," this is usually a reference to an increase in the federal funds rate. Ultimately, this affects consumers in that higher lending costs for banks generally get passed along to their customers. This is natural in that banks generate profit by borrowing money and lending it out to their customers at a higher rate. Consider a mortgage, an automobile loan, and credit cards as common consumer tools that are sensitive to changes in interest rates.

The tricky part of the Fed's job is to make the right decisions about when to raise or lower rates, and by how much. In a sense, the policy makers try to anticipate, based on incoming economic data, what further policy shaping may be necessary. They also take a look at how their prior decisions have been affecting the economy. This is often a difficult thing to do, as a time lag exists between when policy decisions are made and when their effects are disseminated into the economy. If rates remain low for longer than necessary, consumers may be tempted to borrow more than they reasonably can afford to pay back. This can overenergize the economy, resulting in inflation and all of its negative consequences. If rates are kept too high, the economy may slow down more than desired, resulting in a recession. Some have speculated that a target interest rate should exist that the Fed aspires to keep to. While that may sound ideal, many would argue that it's counterproductive to standardize any aspect of the money supply, which is influenced by market factors.

The Fed has other tools it can use to control the money supply as well. The first is altering the reserve requirement—the percentage of cash reserves that member banks must keep on hand. The higher the reserve requirement, the tighter the supply of money will become. The other tool used by the Fed is raising and lowering the discount rate—the interest rate charged to eligible institutions that wish to borrow directly from the Fed.

The reason toying with interest rates tends to be the most popular policy tool used by the Fed is that it's considerably more precise than other measures of controlling the money supply.

Why Does Inflation Matter?

When I was in college, I didn't fully understand the dangers of inflation. It was my feeling that slowing down the economy by tightening interest rates would be potentially more dangerous than a little inflation here and there. This is hardly the case. While inflation may not be of greatest concern for some people, namely those who can raise their prices, consider the number of people who live on fixed incomes. They can't pass higher costs along to anybody else, and therefore they are at risk of not being able to afford necessities such as food and health care.

Do you remember when a can of soda cost 50 cents? 25 cents? Inflation has a way of creeping into our lives slowly and steadily, forcing us to either cut back on purchases or increase our earnings. Inflation also affects the value of our currency. When a dollar buys only 90 cents' worth of goods, it doesn't bode well for foreign investors who speculate on the potential strength of our currency. It may also risk our credibility as a nation when it comes to other countries investing in our government securities. Finally, inflation can be dangerous for our exports if their higher prices cause countries to buy less of our goods and services.

The housing bubble that began taking shape after the stock market pop of 2001 was in many ways the result of a low interest rate environment. Besides the crazy speculation on Internet technology that caused many investors to lose money, we also had the terrorist attacks of September 11, 2001. These two events caused the Fed to worry that an economic slowdown was imminent. It began lowering the federal funds rate until it reached a low of 1 percent in 2003. This was the lowest the rate had been since 1958. This ability to borrow money cheaply, combined with an emerging evolution of risky mortgage products that encouraged people with little or no down payment to buy homes, caused a subsequent increase in demand for housing. Naturally, people overspeculated by purchasing too much real estate without considering factors such as payments and the potential for depreciation. As interest rates climbed back above the 5 percent level, the housing bubble began cooling down and prices quickly stabilized, some more than others. This was an example of an asset bubble being fueled by a low interest rate environment. That being said, the Fed's policy decisions were excellent in retrospect. The country managed to get through 2006 without too much inflation or an economic slowdown.

The stated goal of the Fed to maximize employment is an interesting one, considering that fluctuations in employment figures are a perfectly natural occurrence for any market economy. Full employment, consisting of everyone having a job who wants one, could actually become a dangerous scenario. The Fed, through its monetary policy decisions, affects the employment environment. However, similar to the goal of moderating long-term interest rates, certain employment effects are related to policy decisions that are made to either speed up or slow down the economy. I think the Fed understands that the long-term effects of its monetary policy on employment are minimal. The overall goal is to fend off long-term inflation while smoothing out business cycle volatility in the short run. Even though employment fluctuations are natural, many economists and other individuals still read deeply into employment statistics and use them to make economic predictions.

Does Our Economic System Work?

The concepts behind our national banking system are debated both domestically and internationally. While I tend to be optimistic about the long-term prospects of the U.S. economy, some aren't as confident. I've heard more than once that our generous availability of credit in the United States is dangerous and can lend itself to risky asset bubbles and price volatility. I've also been told that banks shouldn't be allowed to lend out more money than they could cover in the event all of their customers decided to liquidate their funds. This is known as a bank panic, and it happened sporadically throughout the twentieth century. It's a risk faced by market economies, especially those that don't peg their currency to a hard asset such as gold. While some important thinkers still believe the U.S. currency faces major risks of devaluation with the current fiat system, I think the federal government has proved it is capable of achieving economic growth while moderating inflation. I obviously can't speak for the future, but it seems that so far international faith in the dollar has remained stable. I've even heard arguments that economic inequalities are exacerbated by the availability of loose credit. All of these questions lead to other interesting discussions, but nothing we're concerned with at this juncture.

Whereas these are all criticisms that deserve discussion, I still remain confident about the economy looking forward and only moderately concerned about new sets of risks. Our economic policies have consistently fostered growth in the long run, so much so that the United States enjoys a standard of living considerably higher than any other country similar in size.

Finally, I'd like to briefly go over how the Federal Reserve System is set up. The Fed has 12 banks spread out across the United States. These banks are overseen by a board of governors consisting of seven members appointed by the U.S. president. Ben Bernanke is currently the chairman of the Federal Reserve Board, having recently replaced Alan Greenspan. The Fed's Open Market Committee votes on decisions regarding monetary policy such as those discussed earlier. There are 12 members on the committee—the seven Fed governors plus five rotating presidents from the 12 Federal Reserve banks. The Federal Reserve System also includes the member banks, which follow Fed guidelines and participate in the national banking system.

So now you have a clue about what the Fed is and how interest rate decisions could potentially affect your life. Just to recap, these policy decisions do affect you, but at the residual level. The tightening or loosening of monetary policy ultimately trickles down to the consumer level in the form of borrowing costs and the prices of goods and services. I always recommend looking into the interest rate environment before jumping into purchases that may require borrowing money, such as homes and cars.

For More Information

Understanding the impacts of monetary policy will make you a smarter consumer. The blogosphere is certainly a place to learn more about the Fed, its policies, and other economics topics. If you want to read a series of blogs written by experts who actually work at Federal Reserve banks, check out www.chicagofedblogs.org. This is a great opportunity to read candid opinions on topics ranging from regional economic issues to broad macroeconomic issues such as pension reform.

I also like Greg Mankiw's blog (http://gregmankiw.blogspot .com). Greg is a professor at Harvard who writes an economics blog based on his random observations. It's more approachable than some other economics blogs, which could confuse even an economist.

Marginal Revolution (www.marginalrevolution.com) is also a fascinating read and can boast some of the highest traffic of all the economics blogs out there. Part of the reason for that might be the well-diversified topic library, which often stretches beyond the strictly economic arena.

The last one I'll mention is Economist's View (http://economistsview .typepad.com). This blog tackles a lot of macroeconomic issues with a thought-provoking and meticulous approach. The author, Mark Thoma, is a professor at the University of Oregon.

Web Hot Spots

www.federalreserve.gov

www.chicagofedblogs.org

http://gregmankiw.blogspot.com

www.marginalrevolution.com

http://economistsview.typepad.com

24

Life Insurance Is Boring. What Do I Need to Know?

My father recently asked me to price out a term life insurance policy for him. While not entirely necessary, he thought it might be nice to establish a fund, in the event of an untimely death, which would pay for the upkeep and maintenance of his Florida residence. The home has become a family retreat in which we all convene to spend time together and break from the stresses of daily life. His logic is that by earmarking insurance proceeds for the upkeep of the home, we would be more likely to keep the place and visit there after he is gone, rather than selling it and dividing up the proceeds according to his will.

He wanted $500,000 worth of coverage with a level premium over a 15-year term. I began calling around for some quotes. The median price I received was $7,500 per year. I priced out the same policy for myself out of sheer curiosity, and it was $400 per year. One might wonder why such a huge price differential existed between the two policies. Well, 15 years from now would place my father somewhere around 80, about 40 years ahead of where I'll be. Insuring him for 15 years represents a decent-sized risk to the insurance company of having to pay out $500,000. Insuring me represents a much smaller risk.

This is an example of the sort of calculations performed by insurance underwriters and actuaries who help create these policies and ensure that the insurance industry remains profitable. While I always confess that insurance is a boring topic, I find myself somewhat fascinated by this morbid process of creating premiums and spreads based on health risks and mortality tables. I was pleasantly surprised when I priced out a policy for myself and learned that my chances of dying this year are estimated to be below 1 percent.

So what's all the fuss about life insurance? What do you have to know? And how does this all tie into financial planning? The last question is the one I'm most concerned with, followed by how you can determine your life insurance needs and not waste money unnecessarily.

Why Buy a Policy?

Life insurance exists primarily to protect others financially in the event of an untimely death. It can also be used as an estate planning tool. We'll get into these various uses later, but first take the following textbook example in which life insurance would be necessary:

Ted and Fran get married. They are both around 30 years old. As the birth of their first child approaches, Fran decides to take a maternity leave from her day job at a local museum. The couple agrees this is financially possible because Ted was recently promoted after five years working for a real estate firm. Soon after the birth, they move into a new, larger home. Ted supports the family on $150,000 of annual income.

What would happen in this situation if Ted were to die in a sudden tragedy? Assuming neither spouse is independently wealthy, an insurance policy would be crucial. Soon after Ted's passing, Fran would be responsible for making the mortgage payments, car payments, and other daily expenses. While this may be possible for a few months using emergency funds, it is unlikely adequate funding will exist without a substantial policy in place. Ted might also want to provide funding for his child's expenses leading up through college. Because of his young age and excellent health, a term policy with a face value of $850,000 might run him only about $1,500 per year. I would consider this a *necessary* expense for this couple—one they cannot do without.

In the above scenario, the couple may consider taking out a policy for Fran as well. If something happened to her, Ted would suddenly be responsible for childcare expenses in addition to his other costs. His personal savings may not be enough to cover everything.

While these situations are often difficult to talk about, they are very important to understand. Unless you have multiple income sources coming in, adequate savings, and very few people who depend on your ability to earn money, some sort of life insurance policy is usually necessary.

Besides providing for dependents, life insurance can be used to further personal or business interests after death. It's not uncommon for an individual to utilize the proceeds of a policy to establish a legacy with a charity or other nonprofit organization that the person enjoys supporting. Similarly, a business succession plan can be built around an inflow of cash stemming from a life insurance policy. A business owner may have ideas that he is unable to accomplish in his lifetime; by naming the business as a beneficiary, he can ensure that the money is there for others to realize his vision. These are all estate planning ideas that need to be evaluated on an individual basis, but it's important to know that they exist.

What Are My Policy Options?

Once you've concluded on your own that buying a life insurance policy is a good thing to do, how can you decide whether to buy term or whole-life? Term life insurance policies are the simpler choice, offering a stated benefit if the policyholder dies within a set amount of time. Whole-life policies are ongoing and include a savings component that can help build long-term wealth. The question of which is better, like many other financial planning issues, depends almost entirely on your individual situation. If someone were to ask me for an initial reaction to such a question, I would probably recommend looking into term insurance first. The reason is simplicity: Term insurance is cheaper and easier to understand. You determine how much coverage you want and how long you want it for, and the insurance company will spit out how much you need to pay. Regardless of the type of policy you buy, the younger and healthier you are, the lower your premiums will be. If you're like my father in the earlier example, in your 60s with more than a few pounds to lose (sorry, Dad), the policy may be quite a bit pricier.

Whole-life insurance is good for disciplined people who intend to hold their policy for a very long time, often for their "whole life." Unlike term life insurance, whole-life policies have an investment component in addition to the insurance component. Each time a premium payment is made, the portion necessary to cover the insurance cost is deducted first. If any extra premium is left over after insurance and administrative costs, the policy will start building up cash value. Generally, the early years of these policies produce little cash value, as paying for the insurance consumes the majority of the premium. During later years, a larger portion of the premium goes toward the cash value. This is one reason I suggest that a disciplined person is more likely to look into a whole-life policy. If you buy one of these policies and decide not to make any more payments after the first few years, you'll end up without much (if any) cash value, and you could have insured yourself for less money with a term policy.

One added benefit to the fixed account in a whole-life policy is that interest accrues on a tax-deferred basis. One could argue this is a good savings vehicle for people who are passionate about their insurance needs but not so responsible about their savings. This type of policy could kill two birds with one stone. As we'll discuss later on, there's always a price tag attached to these sorts of conveniences. In this case it presents itself in the form of higher expenses.

There are variations of whole-life insurance that expand the marketability of the product. For example, universal life policies provide flexibility in the premium amount and face value of the policy. This way, if you don't feel like making a premium payment one year or can't afford to do so, it could be deducted from the remaining cash balance. You'll obviously want to be sure that sufficient funds exist in the cash value of your policy to keep the insurance in place. In addition, if you decide, perhaps after 20 years of owning the policy, that your need for insurance has been reduced, you can adjust the policy from $1,000,000 of coverage down to $500,000, or perhaps less. Keep in mind that each insurance company has different rules and regulations about its universal policies. These are the kinds of details you'd want to map out before making a purchase.

Another interesting choice for whole life insurance is the variable life policy.* To further enhance the owner's flexibility, a variable contract allows the remaining premium after insurance and administration

---

*Earnings will vary with market conditions and your principal may be at risk. All guarantees, including death benefits, are subject to the claims-paying ability of the issuing insurance company. The investment portfolios may expose you to stock market risk, meaning your investment return and principal value will fluctuate so that shares may be worth more or less than your original investment.

costs are deducted to be invested in stocks and bonds. You still have the ability to choose the fixed account, but if you prefer to participate in the markets, you can allocate your money accordingly. The risk you run is that the markets will decline and your cash value will be reduced as a result. It's important to note that the face value of your policy does not change with variable life, as it can with universal life. The primary difference is how the cash balance gets invested.

The ultimate policy in terms of flexibility is variable universal life, often referred to as flexible premium variable life. This policy allows you to adjust the premium paid, change the face value of the policy, and control the investment options applied to your remaining balance. Needless to say, there will be a certain level of expenses present within these policies to cover the costs of insurance, administration, investment options, and policy flexibility—and yes, the broker gets paid as well.

Which One Is Best?

There is much discussion about the benefits and drawbacks of each type of life insurance policy. I've noticed that money managers tend to like term policies the best, while insurance professionals tend to prefer whole-life. Why? Whole-life policies typically have longer lives, possess more complicated parts, and generate more profit for the insurance companies. Term policies tend to be the opposite: simple and cheap. For this reason, some financial planners and money managers will recommend that you buy the least expensive form of term coverage you can find, and invest any extra money that you would have spent on a pricier policy in low-cost mutual funds or a brokerage account. This method will cover your need for life insurance and allow you to save money, only without the added convenience of doing so through one policy.

An insurance sales professional, however, might point out this reality, which I've observed to be true in practice: Many people lack the discipline to set aside money for additional saving and investing. However, if they factor a whole-life insurance premium into their budget as a fixed annual cost, they will always maintain adequate insurance coverage and will automatically save money in the process. This is one of those convenience aspects that may be worthwhile (especially for those who don't have established retirement plans at work), even if it means higher expenses.

So which policy is right for you? Well, maybe none at all. If you're single and nobody depends on your income, you may be able to avoid this expense completely. However, if you have any dependents, major assets, major liabilities, or any number of other personal needs for it, it may be time to start doing research. If you have a financial planner, he or she may be able to help out with this process, especially when it comes to the variable or universal contracts, which are often quite tricky to navigate. Remember to keep your eyes and ears open to make sure you don't get pushed into a particular product that may not be the best one for you. As much as I'd love to say it doesn't happen, people take blind recommendations from insurance professionals all the time that they later come to regret.

You'll want to think carefully about the different advantages to each type of policy and consider how they factor in with your personality and capacity to earn money. For example, I had a client who expected his need for insurance to increase over the next 10 years but would actually be earning less money at that point. We found a policy that allowed him to pay heavy premiums now that would be cut in half within 10 years. The face value of the policy would stay the same forever.

You also want to be careful about choosing the face value of your contract. Some people rely on rules of thumb, such as 10 times your annual income, as a blanket amount of life insurance to take out. This is not a good move from a financial planning perspective. I prefer to see a spreadsheet of estimated expenses that gives consideration to the spouse, children, their spending habits, their personalities, and the like.

Is There Anything Else I Should Know?

Be sure to price out your policies with various insurance providers. It's surprising how much the price of a life insurance policy can vary from one company to the next. It's also important to check the financial stability of the company you decide to go with. There are numerous rating agencies that rank insurance providers as to their ability to pay claims. If you take out a $2 million policy, you want to know that 20 years from now this provider will still be in existence and able to pay out claims.

If you already have a policy, try to review it either every few years or anytime an event happens that could affect your life insurance needs.

When you do review a policy, be sure to consider not just the amount of insurance you have, but also the current beneficiaries named to receive your funds. Imagine getting divorced and having your ex-spouse accidentally receive the proceeds of your policy! It happens frequently, often when people have already remarried, and it would seem beyond reason that the money should go to anybody other than a current spouse. Think about who will receive your insurance proceeds the same way you would your personal savings or a home.

In light of all this talk about life insurance, I think cost consideration is an important point. For all that obtaining a policy doesn't need to be expensive, especially when you are young and healthy, these costs can add up. Often insurance companies will allow premiums to be paid monthly or annually to give the policyholder some payment flexibility. Some of my clients, especially those who are self-employed, pay life, long-term care, health, and auto policies without help from an employer. This often eats up $10,000 or more per year. The point is, it's important to price out your insurance carefully and buy only what you need.

Finally, I urge you understand how your policy works. Too many people buy life insurance with a blind eye. Considering its importance and the fact that it often lasts a lifetime, you should ask your broker any and all questions you have at the time you buy your policy. You should feel comfortable enough that you can call him or her anytime with a need to ask questions or make changes. Along those lines, you should understand why, if it ever happens, your broker or someone else recommends that you revise a policy or transfer it to a new service provider. Although we try to lead trusting lives, we must ask about actions such as exchanging insurance policies, as they can cost the client money and they often bring in a new commission for the broker. In certain circumstances it may be necessary or even cost-effective to do so, but you want to understand why you're making such changes.

For More Information

Lifeinsure.com is an online resource for information and quotes on life insurance. There is a blog on the site that covers basic questions one might ask, along with references to current articles about life insurance. It can be found at http://discussion.lifeinsure.com.

Families.com is a fun site to surf that gives commentary on just about every aspect of family life. It has an insurance blog located at http://insurance.families.com/blog, which deals with all types of insurance policies ranging from life and long-term care to health and auto. I like it because it has multiple authors and posts new articles daily. It also has neat features such as a week in review for people who want a quick recap.

I recently stumbled onto a great site for comparing term life insurance policies. It's www.intelliquote.com. This is just one of a bunch of web sites that will help you compare quotes. They offer other quotes besides life insurance as well.

Web Hot Spots

http://discussion.lifeinsure.com

http://insurance.families.com/blog

www.intelliquote.com

CHAPTER

25

What Do I Need to Know about Retirement?

Americans talk about retirement all the time. Even when I meet with people in their 20s and 30s, I'm regularly making references to retirement age and ensuing lifestyle changes. This can be partially explained by the fact that retirement is a goal that most people have in common. The reason I say most people, as opposed to everyone, is that some people have negative associations with the concept—something we'll talk about later on.

Another reason we discuss retirement so regularly is that we have retirement plans that the government encourages us to contribute to; the IRA, 401(k), and 403(b) are good examples. Because we gain access to those funds without penalty after age 59½, many people assume such an age to be appropriate for a lifestyle change. The same applies to Social Security benefits, which the government starts handing out sometime between ages 62 and 70. While that age seemingly creeps higher every year, many people associate receiving Social Security checks with reaching a point in their lives when they have completed their tenure in the workforce.

This chapter discusses how the retirement landscape has changed from past generations. I also share my feelings about what we are moving toward in the future. You may find that some popular retirement concerns may not even apply to your situation. Finally, I ponder the question of why some people dislike the concept of retirement.

What Has Changed?

Retiring from corporate service in the 1990s could be summed up by the following: You put in 30 years of hard work, and now you are ready to reap the rewards of having a pension that pays out an amount you can actually live on. It wouldn't be uncommon for employees to receive half pay for the remainder of their lives and possibly exercise some stock options distributed many years earlier, which turn out to be quite profitable. I've met plenty of people who were able to retire in particularly good style thanks to the bull market of the 1990s.

Upon retiring, some people choose to downsize and move to areas with lower costs of living. Many retirees are enticed by the appeal of "retirement communities," which are populated by people who often share similar lifestyles. As we'll discuss, many of these communities are currently undergoing changes to appeal more to younger retirees. Here is a list and brief description of the factors playing into the changing retirement landscape. We'll get into more detail about these factors in the next section.

- *Life span.* People currently in their 40s and 50s with normal medical and lifestyle histories are expected to live into their 80s. Healthy young people in their teens and 20s with good genetics could possibly live into their 90s. Contrast this with people born in 1900, when living past age 65 might would be considered an impressive life span. There are multiple explanations for this, ranging from medical and technological advances to improved information about nutrition, diet, and exercise.
- *Corporate pensions and government entitlements.* This is an issue we'll talk about in detail in the following two chapters, so I won't elaborate on it too much here. Pension plans have quickly been disappearing in place of retirement plans with more predictable costs, such as the 401(k). Simultaneously, the government is throwing around ideas to keep the burdened Social Security system solvent in the face of millions of baby boomers preparing to apply for benefits. The bottom line for American workers is that they must begin taking on more individual responsibility for their financial futures. Owning a home, participating in

retirement plans, and having additional personal savings will prove very important in the future.

- *Lifestyle.* Many people, particularly financial planners, put a specific price tag on retirement. Numerous studies have been released in the past five years showing that the traditional image of retirement has evolved into a new form: a second wind, if you will. Some people are remaining in the workforce, only switching professions to work fewer hours and have more leisure time. Retirement communities are changing as well to appeal to a more youthful audience.

- *The ways we earn money.* If we had told our grandparents there would be dot-com billionaires in the twenty-first century, they'd have had no idea what we were talking about. Similarly, it would have been inconceivable even five years ago that one could make a living as a full-time blogger. As we move toward a more technologically advanced society, earning money from home or even remote locations becomes both a realistic and an attractive option.

What Does the Future Hold?

The idea of living longer is perhaps the largest question mark surrounding retirement, benefit payouts, and personal savings. Rather than dwelling on the negative, such as why living longer demands saving more money, I'm going to suggest something more upbeat. Living longer means you have more time to *earn* money! It also allows your existing savings and investments to compound and grow for a longer amount of time. If, in the future, people are reasonably expected to put in 40 to 50 years of work as opposed to 30 to 40 years, having two full careers in one lifetime might not be unusual. This is quite a change from people born at the turn of the twentieth century, who had to plan on retiring at 60 because they might well not be around by 75. Also, it was not a fair assumption that people would be healthy enough in their 60s to continue working and supporting themselves and their families. That assumption, whether or not you realize it, has already changed.

For example, my father is currently considering selling his dental practice. Rather than using the proceeds to support a work-free lifestyle in Florida, he's considering dedicating a chunk of money to starting the photography business he's always dreamed of. Part of this confidence stems from his belief that in the next 10 years, taking him through age 74, he'll be fully capable of working without any health-related interferences. From a financial planning standpoint, I'll have to make some insurance adjustments to help keep him protected, but I respect his optimism and ambition.

We're also seeing a lifestyle evolution for current retirees. This is probably a combination of the other factors already mentioned along with an expectation of longer life expectancies. Certain people who are able to retire at 60 prefer to ease into it rather than to abruptly stop working. I like to refer to this as a "transitional retirement," in which, rather than ceasing work completely, one can put in fewer hours either at the same job or in a different profession. Because, presumably, most people have already put aside some money toward the future, leisure time can be factored into an annual routine (and budget). Maintaining even a partial stream of income will help slow down the depletion of retirement assets, whether through less frequent withdrawals or by avoiding extracting money from a home. Perhaps most important, part-time work keeps the mind and body active, two important factors in actually reaching those longer life expectancies.

The communities that exist to house retirees have been evolving as well. So-called active lifestyle communities are not a brand-new concept. However, they have become quite popular lately. If you have a chance to visit a relative or friend living in one of these communities, see if it reminds you of summer camp. There are event schedules, activities directors, clubhouses, dining facilities, and communal transportation. The idea is to keep people living for as long as possible in a fun and energetic setting. These communities are popping up all over the place, rather than just in areas with warm climates. This corresponds to the desire of people to work part-time in addition to enjoying their leisure activities. Most of these developments seek residents as young as their late 50s and up. Some of the more traditional retirement communities are filled mostly with people in their 70s, an age that turns off younger retirees looking for people in their age range.

Finally, technology is having a big impact on retirement options. One reason people had to make absolute decisions about retirement in the 1960s, 1970s, and 1980s was that working from home or some other isolated area was not a possibility. Nowadays, thanks to e-mail, instant messaging, video messaging, personal digital assistants (PDAs), Internet telephone, and remote desktops, it's hard not to get blasted with information. More people than ever are finding ways to generate side income either from Web-based businesses or from work they can do from home. This lends itself to part-time retirement work, especially for people who don't feel like getting dressed and driving to work.

Why Do Some People Dislike Retirement?

One thing I've learned through my involvement in the financial planning industry is that many people don't consider retirement to be the ultimate financial goal. When asked about what age they wish to stop working, many clients reply that stopping work is not of particular concern to them. Nearly everyone has in common that they want to live in the place of their choice without worrying about money; however, the idea of working, at least in some capacity, is often not rejected.

An explanation for this, whether or not the client realizes, is that retirement often implies a certain level of isolation. I know several people who have moved elsewhere after retiring, often where the weather is warm, to begin a life filled with reading, writing, hobbies, and relaxation. I've heard, generally within one year of retiring, some desire to begin working again or increase their interaction with people on a daily basis. The extent to which retirement is a big transition is often understated and should be explained better to people who assume it's what they want.

I've often pondered what would happen if we eliminated the word *retirement* completely in place of some other, more fitting terminology. I happen to like "phase two" or "graduation." I have positive associations with some of these words, whereas retirement, pardon my honesty, reminds me of the final phase of life. I understand this is a somewhat unrealistic expectation that would become problematic for governments and corporations that utilize the term each day. It would probably also confuse my clients, many of whom are working toward this retirement goal. If they were all of a sudden working toward "graduation" instead, I'd have a lot of explaining to do. Nevertheless, I look forward to the evolution in the retirement landscape, in whatever form it takes. I have high expectations for the globalized world to work together toward living, rather than dying.

For More Information

When I first started looking into retirement blogs I wasn't sure what to expect. There had been only a small handful that I'd seen or heard about through my usual blogging circles. Surprisingly, there's a plethora of blogs out there dealing with retirement planning issues. Take So Baby Boomer, for example, a financial planning blog geared toward baby boomers expecting to live long and healthy lives. It can be found through a link at http://coachingtip.blogs.com.

Along the same lines, check out GenPlus at http://genplus.blog spot.com. The founder, Wendy, hopes to shed some light on "jobs, love, and life at age 50+." I also like the Boomer Chronicles, found at www .thegeminiweb.com. This blogger has a great sense of humor, which she integrates into her explorations of life's realities after age 40.

The National Council on Aging has put together a great resource at www.benefitscheckup.com. It matches up people age 55 or older with the benefits to which they are entitled. Ironically, many people in need of assistance either aren't aware of certain benefits or have no clue how to gain access to them. This site will navigate through existing federal, state, and local programs for you. I think it's worth a visit.

Web Hot Spots

http://coachingtip.blogs.com
http://genplus.blogspot.com
www.thegeminiweb.com
www.benefitscheckup.com

What Are My Chances of Getting Social Security?

Social Security is a federal program that provides retirement and disability income to workers through the collection of Social Security taxes. All workers in the United States are responsible for paying these taxes during their working years and are entitled to receive benefit checks when they are eligible for retirement. That fact alone should make you at least a little bit curious about what all the recent chatter is about.

The program is on its way to financial trouble because not enough workers exist to provide adequate benefits to the rapidly aging population. The most perplexing aspect of the Social Security problem is that the people who are most concerned about it really aren't the same people who will likely be most affected by it.

For example, I'm the youngest financial adviser at my firm and stand to lose the most from an underfunded Social Security system. At the same time, I not only talk about it less than my co-workers, but I don't lose sleep over it, either. That's not to say I'm unaware that 12.4 percent of my paycheck goes toward these taxes; I'm just too far from receiving benefits to worry about it.

Perhaps part of that irresponsible logic stems from how the system is organized. Rather than each taxpayer's Social Security dollars getting earmarked for the worker's own retirement, they get paid into a common pool of money to be allocated by the federal government. It's a controversial system because workers currently in their 20s and

30s may not ever see the money they've paid in. It's also impractical because millions of baby boomers will soon be retiring and applying for benefits at the same time. This will put an unusually large strain on the system.

The irony of this problem is that Social Security was set up in part as a reaction to the Great Depression. Its inherent purpose was to provide a safe and stable income during retirement. When the Federal Insurance Contribution Act (FICA) was passed in 1937, the payroll tax needed to fund the system was only 2 percent, not a bad deal for a promise of secure income during retirement. Needless to say, that payroll tax has increased gradually up to its current 12.4 percent level. If we consider the other 2.9 percent in Medicare tax included in FICA withholding, we're up to a steep 15.3 percent of wages.*

Some politicians may finally be realizing that raising taxes isn't necessarily the solution. It's more than questionable what the effects would be of raising FICA taxes another few percentage points. Some believe that sort of action would infuriate many hardworking people, potentially risking a shake-up in the economy. It seems to me that the system makes less sense each and every year it continues.

So, what are we to do about all this? Keep in mind throughout this discussion that eliminating the Social Security system along with the taxes that fund it is not an option currently on the table. The government understands that it needs to implement, at least in the short run, a uniform program that provides some form of income to older Americans.

What Are the Solutions?

There are a few solutions currently being entertained by politicians that would allow the system to remain in place and, at the very least, delay the lurking problems for another few decades. Here they are, along with a brief opinion about each of the ideas.

Raise the Payroll Tax

We've been trying this for about 70 years. It just doesn't seem to work. It postpones the problem and costs us money in the interim. More important, raising taxes can probably never be the permanent solution because a lack of tax dollars isn't the root of the problem.

---

*FICA taxes are applied to only the first $97,500 in earnings, up from $94,200 in 2006.

A more accurate prediction of demographic shifts is really what we need in order to properly assess the Social Security shortfall. If our temporary solutions don't address the right problems, they'll probably fail and become an issue again for our children and grand-children. Needless to mention, the concept of raising taxes doesn't exactly get workers excited.

Raise the Retirement Age

Technically, you may begin receiving reduced Social Security ben-efits as early as 62 years of age. However, there are a bunch of annoy-ing requirements you must satisfy to qualify for such a benefit. The age at which the system intends for us to take benefits, and doesn't penalize us for doing so, is known as the full retirement age. The full retirement age varies depending on when you are born (65 years old for those born before 1938, increasing gradually for those born in later years). The official Social Security web site (www.ssa.gov) speci-fies it to be 67 years old for those born after 1960.

The full retirement age is the age politicians are referring to when they suggest raising the retirement age as a solution to an underfunded Social Security system. I don't see much of a point to this solution since it's really just a reduction in benefits. For ex-ample, let's hypothesize that raising the retirement age for those born after 1960 to 69 years old (from the currently specified age 67) would add 25 years of liquidity to the Social Security system. That would cost a person whose benefit would be $1,600 per month a total of $38,400 over those two years. So, all we really did was cut the benefit.

Frankly, I'd rather see FICA taxes go up slightly than see a reduction in benefits. To raise the retirement age or reduce benefits doesn't seem to be a solution, rather an admission of failure. Plus, it discriminates against those who paid their fair share and will have to work more years to receive their benefits. I reject this solution along with raising taxes.

Reduce Other Federal Spending Programs

When I first heard about this solution I thought it sounded reason-able. We rearrange our priorities such that providing retirement income requires a greater percentage of our federal budget. Perhaps we can spend 1 percent less on the military and apply it to Social

Security. If not the military, could we try reducing federal spending on education? Or maybe eliminate the Environmental Protection Agency?

Do you see the problem here? Our federal budget is already stretched out like Silly Putty, and interest accrues on the money we borrow. If we cut something like subsidized housing projects to provide more Social Security dollars, it ultimately just becomes an equally expensive problem for workers. We can talk about altering federal spending to increase Social Security funding, but I can't really see it happening. Politicians already disagree on nearly every piece of spending that Congress considers. If the solution to the Social Security problem becomes a shift of the problem to a different sector of the economy, it may as well not be implemented in the first place. Thus, I throw this idea away as the full solution to the problem but believe shifts in federal spending are inevitable and could be helpful in the process.

Create Private Accounts for Each Participant

In my opinion, setting up private accounts is the only solution currently on the table that makes sense. Yes, there are reasons why this solution is problematic, but let's entertain why it may work. The idea entails a portion (not the whole 12.4 percent, but a portion) of your FICA taxes to be deferred into a private account earmarked just for you. You (the individual worker) then determine whether you want the money invested conservatively, moderately, or aggressively. This provides the potential for your money to grow at a rate much faster than the current system, where funds are invested in ultrasafe Treasury securities. Consider the fact that from January 1926 through September 2006 the annualized total return for the S&P 500 index was 10.44 percent.* If our FICA taxes were growing at this rate, we probably wouldn't have the Social Security issue on the table yet.

The obvious concern would be that the stock market might not perform at the rate it has for the past 100 years. Social Security was set up to provide stability, not a fluctuating investment that could possibly be worth less than what you originally put in.

Just the amount of debate and interest this solution has created lends credibility to it. The heart of the issue is whether individual

---

*www2.standardandpoors.com.

workers are capable of taking personal responsibility for a portion of their Social Security income. Further, is it safe to let inexperienced investors make decisions about how their Social Security funds should be allocated? Are Americans, overall, competent enough to make decisions about these sorts of things? Keep in mind that the private accounts aren't intended to totally eliminate the government's inter-action. The government would still, theoretically, create the program, set up the investment options, and provide some form of investor education.

Again, this whole concept is hotly debated and there is no way of knowing how the system would work in practice. What we do know is that before long the current system won't work. We also know that an S&P 500 index fund would have, over the past 80 years, provided a much higher rate of return than Treasury securities.

What Do Professionals Think?

I've read up on professional opinions regarding the establishment of private accounts for the Social Security system, and they vary widely. This would make sense considering it's nearly impossible to predict the events of the next 50 years. That being said, those with solid backgrounds in economics can hypothesize to some extent the sort of problems that are likely to occur.

Bill Gross, manager of one of the largest mutual funds, feels that Social Security imbalances are curses of demographics and not financial funding.* He feels a refocusing on the causes of the Social Security problem could influence our choice of solutions.

Ralph Nader, the consumer advocate and former presidential candidate, believes that the Social Security problem is "overstated" and the use of "pessimistic assumptions" taints the reality of the problem.[†] Furthermore, he has advocated against privatization as he feels it would be dangerous because of stock market fluctuation and investment fraud.

Our current president, George W. Bush, is a strong advocate of private accounts, pushing hard for them during his second-term agenda. It is looking, however, like the American public is not ready to dramatically alter a system that is so fundamental to our lives.

---

*http://money.cnn.com/2005/02/04/markets/gross_social_security/index.htm.
[†]www.ontheissues.org/2004/Ralph_Nader_Social_Security.htm.

For More Information

The Internet is loaded with resources for learning more about Social Security. For sheer accuracy and to avoid partisan politics, I would recommend a visit to the official web site of the U.S. Social Security Administration (www.ssa.gov).

After you get the cold, hard facts, the blogosphere will certainly help you form your own opinion about the matter. Because the topic has political undertones and blogs originated in the political arena, there's a surplus of sites having a similar discussion to the one we've had in this chapter. I'm going to reference only authoritative sites that truly stick to the issues.

Social Security Choice (www.socialsecuritychoice.org) is a major proponent of reform and promotes the establishment of individual accounts on its blog. It is part of a larger organization called the Club for Growth, which believes that prosperity and opportunity come through economic freedom.

S4: Students for Saving Social Security (www.secureourfuture. org) is a site created by students for students to spread the word about how Social Security issues affect them. As I mentioned in the first part of the chapter, younger workers will ultimately shoulder the burden of national debts, Social Security and otherwise, more than workers nearing retirement.

You may also wish to visit the Social Security blog located at http://blog.pactamerica.com/. PactAmerica is another organization dedicated to practical Social Security reform. They have a variety of interesting links and should be full of updates as the 2008 presidential election gets closer.

We don't know at this point what the right answer is. What we do know is that a problem is brewing, and avoiding it could jeopardize our retirement benefits.

Web Hot Spots

www.ssa.gov

www.socialsecuritychoice.org

www.secureourfuture.org

http://blog.pactamerica.com

27

What Is This Pension Crisis I Keep Hearing about, and How Will It Affect My Retirement?

Y ou may have noticed an increase recently in media coverage regarding problems with corporate pension plans. There has been a trend toward reducing, if not completely terminating, certain benefits that provide security and peace of mind for millions of workers. The problem, in a nutshell, is that corporations are having trouble predicting future pension liabilities and therefore are turning to more cost-predictable retirement plans, such as the 401(k).

There are three key questions that must be answered when discussing the pension crisis.

1. What created the current crisis?
2. Is my pension or retirement plan at risk?
3. How can I protect myself from the possibility of future reductions in benefits?

Answering the latter two questions requires poking around a bit in your own workplace and assessing where you may become vulnerable.

Discussing the potential economic consequences of the pension crisis enables you to make better decisions in your financial life, such as better determining how much money to save through other retirement plans and savings vehicles.

What Is the Pension Crisis?

Simply put, the pension crisis is the expectation that insufficient funds will be available to cover companies' future pension liabilities. Similar to the Social Security problem, it has proved difficult to forecast factors such as the future earnings of a company, the life spans of employees currently receiving pension benefits, and the future investment returns earned by pension managers.

Funding issues have been most prevalent in cyclical industries such as automobiles, airlines, and steel. In fact, the Employee Retirement Income Security Act (ERISA), the legislation regulating private-sector retirement plans, is believed by many to have originated in response to the 1963 collapse of automaker Studebaker Corporation, which left 11,000 workers with terminated pension benefits. The economic explanation for this was very logical. The automobile industry is a lesson in bad economics. Automakers experience stiff competition, rising commodity prices, and heavy fixed costs. All of these factors bode ill for long-term pension obligations. This wasn't always the case; automobile manufacturers were the darlings of the economy in the 1950s and 1960s. The crisis began when corporations could not afford to pay out the promised level of benefits and needed to figure out a way to make up for the shortfall.

Prior to 1974, no governmental body existed to help remedy pension funding issues. As part of the ERISA legislation, the Pension Benefits Guarantee Corporation (PBGC) was established. The goal of the PBGC is to help maintain private-sector pension plans. It does so by taking over terminated pension plans and continuing to pay out their benefits, up to certain maximums, using a combination of remaining plan assets and funds garnered by the PBGC through insurance premiums and investment returns. It has proved to be a crucial organization, although one that runs with substantial deficits ($22.8 billion as of November 15, 2005).*

Are Your Retirement Funds at Risk?

First of all, do you have a pension where you work? If so, what guarantees are in place that you'll receive it? If you have a public service job (e.g., teacher, police officer, or government employee), you don't really have reason to sweat—at least not yet. These pensions

---

*www.house.gov/list/press/ed31_democrats/rel111505b.html.

are contractual obligations of the states (which have the power to tax) and are most likely to be paid. It's the private sector that needs to be on higher alert.

The first thing you can do is ask your boss or human resources director about the financial health of your pension. Don't be shy about asking a question that would never be expected to come from you. When talking about your own future, it's very important that you know the full story. If you have trouble finding out about the specifics of your pension, don't worry too much about it. The goal is to get an idea of what your promised level of benefits are, and how likely you are to receive them. You may already get an annual update regarding the status of your pension benefits, but you may soon start getting better and more complete information. The Pension Protection Act, passed in 2006, has a multitude of provisions designed for keeping employees in the loop about their retirement benefits.

Once you get past the pension questions, look into other retirement plans. In the public sector, you may have a 403(b) or 457 plan, while the private sector typically utilizes 401(k) plans. Unlike most pensions, the majority of funds that go into all these types of plans are your own. They are deducted automatically from your paycheck and self-directed into the investment choices offered by the plan. The amount of risk you face depends entirely on how you decide to allocate your money. You can leave it all in conservative funds that are aimed at earning interest, or you can put the money into more aggressive investments that seek out stocks with appreciation potential. While the allocation of your self-directed retirement accounts should be created around your risk tolerance, I can offer a few tips. First, most people can tolerate more volatility in their portfolios when they are younger. A typical allocation will be more aggressive through the account owner's 30s and 40s, and gradually transition out of stocks and into more conservative investments upon hitting one's 50s and 60s. Remember, this is a rule of thumb and depends largely on your personal risk tolerance. If you have millions of dollars saved up, you may wish to keep a larger percentage of your funds invested in stocks as you get older. Another good idea for retirement plans is to avoid tax-free bonds and other similar investments with lower returns. Tax-friendly investments lose their appeal because growth and income in retirement plans such as the 401(k) and 403(b) are not subject to taxes until withdrawn anyway.

Private-sector employees will probably see more buzz about 401(k) plans in the future as the number of corporations that offer pensions and other defined-benefit plans continues to shrink. My personal feeling is that even public pensions will eventually be reduced or eliminated, as the problems surrounding the pension system are not specific to corporations. The underlying issues deal with actuarial assumptions about the economy and population statistics. These assumptions are extremely difficult to make, and even conservative estimates can be problematic. As a result, it becomes more practical for employers to offer defined-contribution plans such as the 401(k). If the employer includes features such as matching funds, the plan will remain appealing while keeping costs within reason and improving the ability to plan for future expenses.

Here's an interesting example of a situation that could prove disastrous for pension liabilities. What if science reaches a point in the next 50 years in which the average life expectancy becomes 98 years old? If a person retires at age 62, is the former employer responsible for paying out 36 years of benefits? I can't imagine that even profitable organizations could prepare for that sort of financial liability.

What Can You Do to Protect Your Retirement?

In the interest of protecting your retirement, regardless of whether you receive a pension, you'll want to know which retirement plans you're eligible for. The first question is whether you have a pension plan, or similar defined-benefit plan, available to you at work. The next question should be which *additional* retirement plans, namely defined-contribution plans, are available to you. Whether or not you are eligible for a pension, you should still investigate these other plan possibilities. For example, many corporations offer 401(k) plans. While this retirement vehicle is fairly common, you may also have a profit-sharing plan available to you after you've reached a certain rung on the corporate ladder. Ask your employer these types of questions so that you can plan with the best information possible.

Keep in mind that you can still retire in style without qualifying for a pension plan. A pension is just something you need to know about so you can plan around it. For example, if you don't have a pension, you'd probably be more concerned about maximizing contributions to other savings vehicles. As a general rule about saving for retirement, try to utilize plans that provide tax benefits *before* any other individual saving or investing you may do. If you're passing up an opportunity for tax-deferred growth, you should have a good reason for doing so.

Once you figure out which plans are available, try to *quantify* how much those plans will be worth to you. With pensions, the amount of retirement benefits one is eligible for generally varies based on factors such as retirement age, years of service, salary, and when benefits are taken. If an employee figures out that $40,000 is that individual's approximate pension benefit each year, that information will make calculations for other savings and investments easier to quantify. Perhaps your goal is to have $60,000 per year to spend during retirement. If you will receive $40,000 through the pension, you need to accumulate enough money through other sources to provide $20,000 per year for the rest of your estimated life span. Careful planning, either on your own or with a good financial planner, should help you more accurately make these calculations.

One other important detail is figuring out what percentage of retirement benefits you're entitled to and when. For example, a government pension plan may agree to pay out 50 percent of your salary every year for the rest of your life upon reaching age 55, as long as you have put in 25 years of service. However, what if, after 22 years of service, you start to dislike some of your co-workers and think maybe you'd be better off taking an early retirement? This scenario could prove dangerous if you're leaving just prior to reaching eligibility for the majority of your benefits. It is common for employees to get burnt out before they qualify for the highest benefit thresholds, and they often force themselves to stay at work so they don't miss out. A great example of this is teaching, where a contract will frequently lay out the optimum table for retirement. Sometimes a cash incentive is offered if you agree to retire in the year you qualify for retirement. This helps the system make better cost predictions and bring in lower-paid employees.

I've also seen people miss out on large sums of money because they don't understand *when* their benefits become payable. For example, there are often vesting schedules attached to retirement dollars. Vested funds already belong to you when you leave your employer. One might encounter vested funds in a profit-sharing plan or in the company-match portion of a 401(k) plan. Part of the reason employers establish vesting schedules is to retain employees. By vesting benefits after five years or so, an employer can more accurately predict employee turnover. This accuracy filters down to other areas of business operation as well. Vesting schedules are usually reasonable because they provide a compromise for both employers and employees. If you have a compensation plan like this at your workplace, take the time to understand how the benefits get paid. Also, try not to switch jobs the year before you vest into a plan. If you need help sorting through the plan documents, give them to your adviser for help.

What Are the Potential Economic Consequences of a Pension Crisis?

The pension crisis could affect you—even if you aren't entitled to a pension. While it may seem unfair, the only reasonable solution to the pension crisis may be for taxpayers to bear the burden. Most of the other suggested solutions involve the affected employees taking drastic reductions in benefits, presumably forcing them into a position of financial hardship. (How would you react to spending 30 years working for the same company and then learning your benefits may become unavailable?)

   The problem facing the Social Security system has similar roots. It has proved very difficult to determine accurate economic and demographic assumptions that can be used to forecast future funding needs. The pension issue is worse for taxpayers in a sense because, while everyone theoretically is entitled to a Social Security check, not everyone gets a pension check. Angry taxpayers, especially in the private sector, will undoubtedly point out this inequality when asked to take on some of the burden. They must remember that a major part of the government's function is to find reasonable solutions to problems while minimizing the effects of those problems on the broader economy. If the pension problem can be solved while avoiding negative externalities such as poverty and increased income inequality, the government has done its job.

   In the grand scheme of things, I don't consider the pension crisis as problematic as some other domestic and global issues. However, it is a problem that continues to get worse as time passes. The pension problem won't initially default to the federal government. The first organization to feel the financial strain will be the PBGC, which exists primarily to mitigate problems such as underfunding that affect pension benefits. Some plans may have only a small need for assistance, while other plans, which go through *distress termination*, may have shortfalls running well into the billions. My deepest worries about the pension crisis are for the future, when we could potentially see larger and more rapid rates of default. This could send the PBGC searching for an amount of money only a governmental body could provide.

Some have speculated that pension managers could possibly make up the shortfalls by averaging higher rates of return on investments. I don't think this is a realistic possibility. To take on the level of risk needed to create a financial surplus would be a dangerous thing to do with retirement funds. If the added risks didn't work out as planned, the problem could become even deeper. What's more likely is that the federal government will become more conservative with pension guidance by creating stricter requirements for pension funding going forward. Meanwhile, solutions, perhaps involving your tax dollars, may be needed to keep the PBGC solvent. A new piece of legislation signed into law in 2006 has already started tackling the pension problem. The Pension Protection Act aims to reform the pension system in the most major overhaul since ERISA.

For More Information

This chapter should give you a better grasp of the pension issue. A visit to the Web can further engage your curiosity regarding either general pension issues or more specific information such as which corporations are already strapped for cash. The pension crisis is a hot topic, and I've noticed the conversation continue to broaden from a general discussion on pensions to one that includes the PBGC (www. pbgc.gov), current federal legislation, and criticism of past policy decisions.

You can visit www.benefitslink.com if you want to participate in ongoing discussions regarding retirement plans. This is one place I turn to for answers to specific questions that require an expert's review. Usually one or two gurus are crawling through these discussion boards, sharing wisdom with the rest of us.

The www.plansponsor.com web site is a great resource as well. It is easy to navigate and has all sorts of great features. Among my favorites are the available NewsDash, which is a morning e-mail briefing on events that could affect plan sponsors and their participants, and the plan sponsor blog, which can be found at http:// plansponsorinstitute.blogspot.com.

Some other excellent blogs that touch on the pension crisis and related topics are www.retirementplanblog.com and http://fiduciaryinvestor.blogspot.com/.

Web Hot Spots

www.pbgc.gov

www.benefitslink.com

www.plansponsor.com

www.plansponsorinstitute.blogspot.com

www.retirementplanblog.com

http://fiduciaryinvestor.blogspot.com/

Index